The Flov … waledale

Jocelyn M. Campbell

HAYLOFT PUBLISHING LTD

First published by Hayloft Publishing Ltd., 2014

Hayloft Publishing Ltd, South Stainmore,
Kirkby Stephen, Westmorland, CA17 4DJ

tel: 017683 41568 or 07971 352473
email: books@hayloft.eu
web: www.hayloft.eu

ISBN 978 1 910237 03 8

A CIP record for this book is available from The British Library

Designed, printed and bound in the EU

Papers used by Hayloft are natural, recyclable products made from wood grown in sustainable forests. The manufacturing processes conform to the environmental regulations of the country of origin.

This book is dedicated to the memory of
Grace Buckle, with gratitude.
She loved Swaledale, and its Flora and Fauna.

Contents

Preface

FOR many years I have considered that an understanding and the enjoyment of the Dales landscapes familiar to visitor and strong walker alike, are enhanced by close observation 'of the ground beneath our feet' or rather the woods, trees and flowers which grow beneath our feet. Jocelyn has recently published her closely observed drawings of the woodland landscapes and the trees and has now made available her strong portraits of many of the flowers to be seen at different localities within the Dale.

This work is not a botanical flora of Swaledale – no such flora yet exists, rather a selection of watercolours which reflect the personality and evolutionary characteristics of each flower seen through the eyes of an artist as though painting commissioned portraits.

It is no small achievement that the watercolours are both botanically accurate and artistic portraits. From my own point of view these portraits will encourage me to observe each plant even more closely, with *Collins Flower Guide* in hand and Sowerby's twelve volumes of his *English Botany* for refence at home on the shelf.

The absence of a formal flora of Swaledale is to be regretted. It is greatly to be hoped that this collection of flower paintings will motivate a competent botanist to set about the fieldwork necessary and provide the formal record of the vegetation of the varied landscapes of Swaledale and Arkengarthdale.

This will be no small task as the most interesting localities are the high limestone scars, the riverside woods and remote waterfall ravines at the head of the many tributary becks. All these locations are inaccessible to sheep and to all but the bravest of people alike.

Jocelyn has painted many flowers which are widespread and familiar. A few of the flowers painted are uncommon and also several are rare flowers which now survive only at these interesting but difficult places or in pastures and at wet spring flushes which have not been 'improved', drained or planted with trees.

Tim Laurie, May 2014

Introduction

THE intention in producing this book is to help people who visit, or live in Swaledale and Arkengarthdale, to identify some of the diverse wild flowers which grow there. The mixed habitats in the dales, between high moorland to lush valleys, from acid to alkaline soils, and the different exposures to the northern climate, produce a rich variety of flowers.

Thanks to the efforts of individual farmers and the Yorkshire Dales National Park, and to the age-old methods of agriculture, there remains a richness enviable to many areas. The hay meadows are legendary. Here hay is the only crop harvested, and fields have never been ploughed or re-seeded. The abundance of wild flowers amongst the grass produces a tapestry of colour each summer, which brings admirers from everywhere. The carpets of buttercups, although not very popular with farmers, bring photographers from the national press to share the beauty with outsiders.

No one will forget the sight in spring of the lush growth along the dale roads. Cow parsley and sweet cecily burst into a lacy froth of white, with purple geraniums, strong smelling ransoms, bluebells, campanulas, primroses and foxgloves, transforming the dales.

As summer advances the dramatic purple on the moor tops, when the heather scents the air, and finally the blaze of willowherb, or fireweed, with its splashes of vivid pink, gradually brings the floral outburst to an end. The rust bracken and golden marsh grasses, even the blackening heather as winter descends, still have a visual appeal which is special to the Pennines. The landscape may change to a spider's web of black walls and stark trees and cliffs, but we know that as the first spring days arrive the flowers are waiting to burst colourfully for another year.

All this glory is protected by the Yorkshire Dales National Park policies in preserving the flora and fauna. Farmers are encouraged to leave mowing the hay until the flower seeds are set so that they can propagate naturally. Natural habitats, control of moor drainage, planting of trees, are all encouraged. Picking of wild flowers is forbidden. Our local school children are encouraged to study and value this floral heritage. This book, therefore, only indicates the habitats where certain flowers are likely, the exact locations are not given.

The flowers are seen through the eye of the artist, not a botanist, but will hopefully be how others observe and can identify them. The intention in producing this book is to give pleasure to visitors and others by helping them to see and preserve this special beauty of our dales. For exact botanical details a general book on the flora of Britain may be needed.

Jocelyn M. Campbell
March 2014

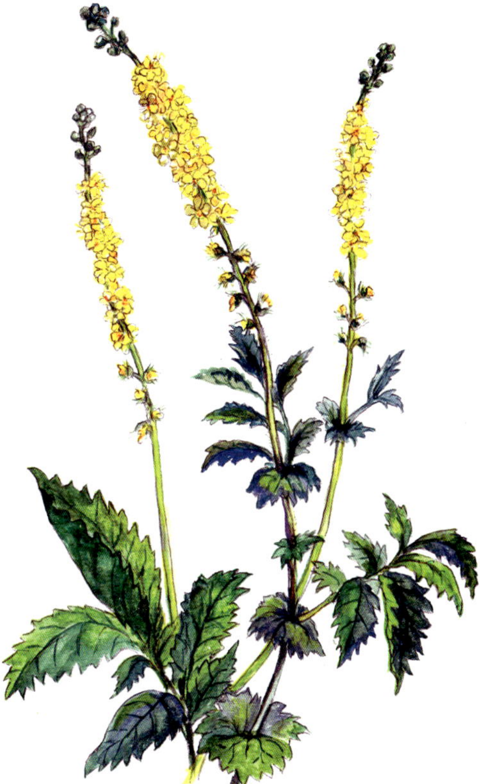

AGRIMONY

Agrimonia eupatoria *Family ROSACEAE*

These small, yellow flowers with five petals, grow the length of spiky stems. The plant has graceful leaves along its stems, diminishing in size at the tip. It was thought at one time to be a cure for snake bites.

Flowers June to August.

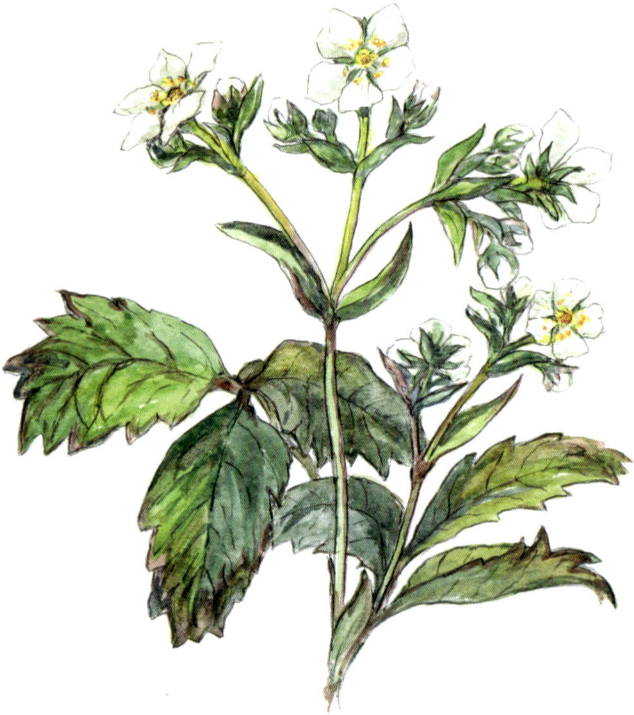

BARREN STRAWBERRY

Potentilla sterilis *Family ROSACEAE*

Unlike many Dales plants, it prefers dry soil. It is a smaller plant than the wild strawberry, has bluish leaves and hairy stems, and a white flower. It is one of the earliest flowers to appear.

Flowers February to May.

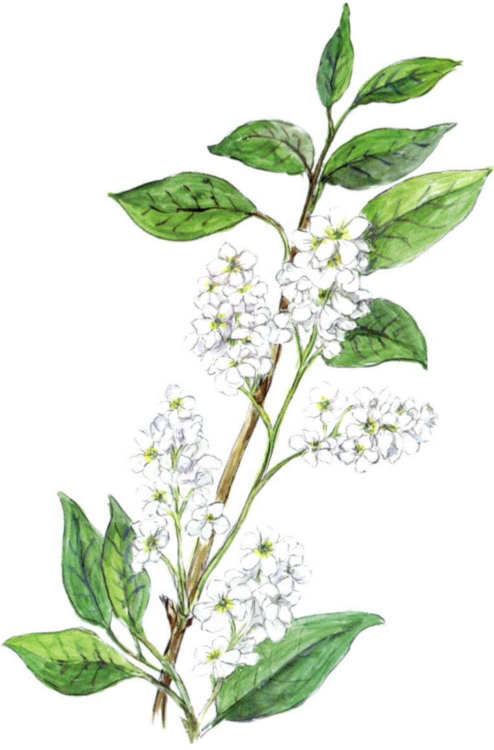

BIRD CHERRY.

Prunus padus *Family ROSACEAE*

This is a tall shrub or tree and thrives in woods and waterfall ravines inaccessible to grazing animals. Although it is said to be rare, it is known in the north and in Scotland. It has an abundance of sweet-smelling white flowers which cluster along the end of the branches in spikes, which sometimes hang down. The black fruits are liked by birds in spite of their bitterness.

Flowers April to May.

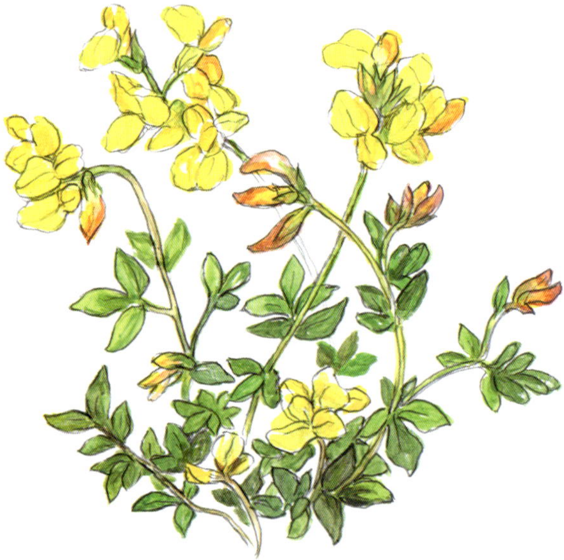

BIRDSFOOT TREFOIL
(Eggs and bacon, Lady's slipper, Tom thumb)
Lotus corniculatus *Family LEGUMINOSAE*

With bright yellow pea-shaped flower, red markings and clover-like oval leaves, this is one of the commonest little plants on dry or bare ground throughout the valley and hillsides.

Flowers May to September.

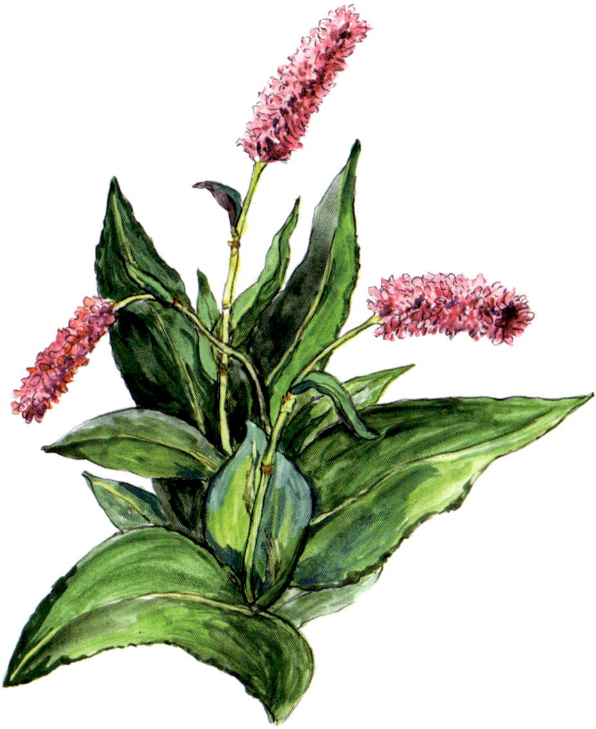

BISTORT
(Snakeweed)

Polygonum bistorta *Family POLYGONACEAE*

This unbranched plant makes a fine show in clumps in marshy places, or near streams. It has large smooth leaves and small bright pink flowers, which form a compact spike at the end of each stem. It grows to at least eighteen inches tall. It is more common in the north of the country than in the south.
Flowers June to August.

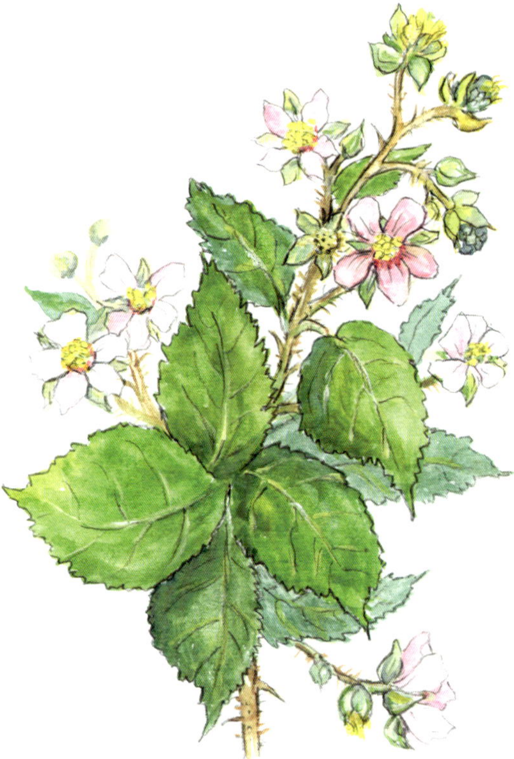

BLACKBERRY

Rubus fruticosus *Family ROSACEAE*

This is a prickly shrub which clambers over hedgerows, and in late summer produces the delicious berries which we use for cooking, jam and jelly. The flowers have five white to pink petals, and the berries start green, turning to shiny black. It grows commonly along the dale's roadsides and hedges.

Flowers from June.

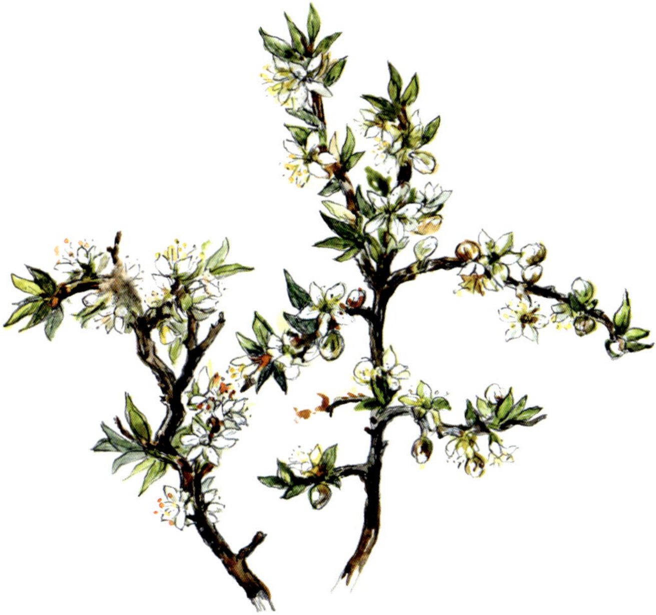

BLACKTHORN

Prunus spinosa *Family ROSACEAE*

One of the first shrubs to appear on the hillsides and hedges with a burst of white blossom, which stands out against the nearly leafless dark branches. The leaves appear fully once the flowers are over. This shrub produces the small plum/sloe berry, very bitter to taste unless mixed with gin and sugar, or made into a jelly.

Flowers April to May.

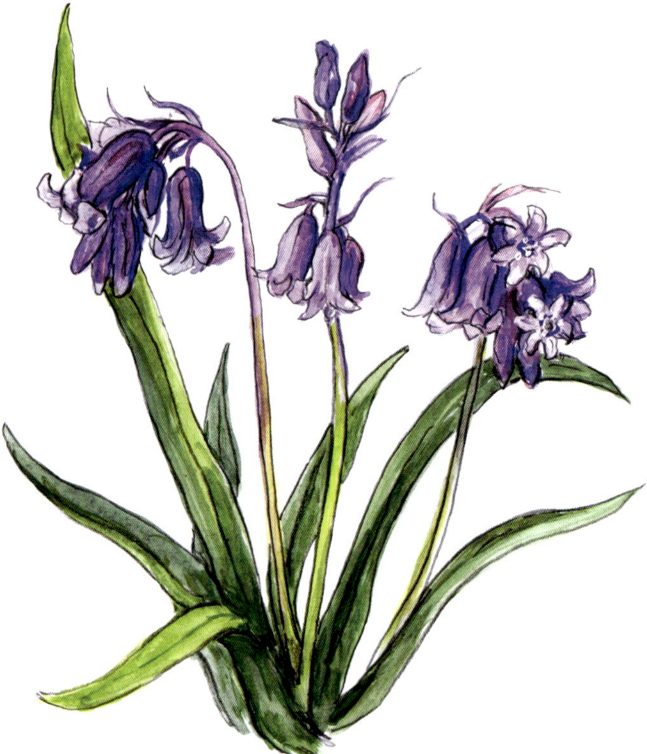

BLUEBELL

Endymion non-scriptus *Family LILIACEAE*

Swathes of sweet smelling blue flowers, so well known in our woodlands, can be surprisingly, found on quite high hillsides among more typical moorland flora. These patches have been left behind when the woods which once covered the dale hillsides vanished.

Flowers April to May

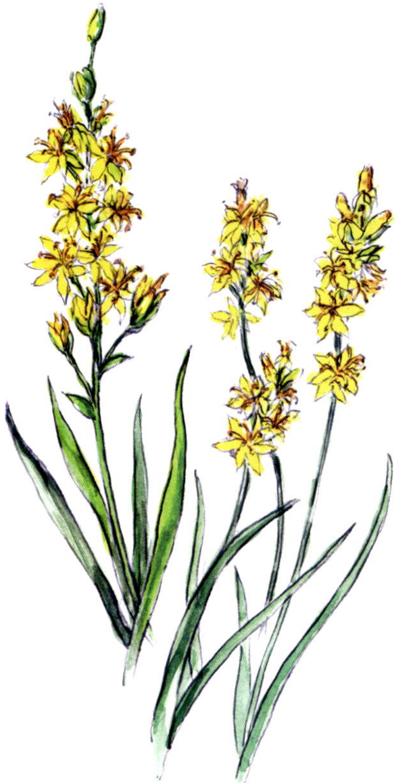

BOG ASPHODEL

Narthecium ossifragum *Family NARTHECIACEAE*

This small plant with narrow sword shaped leaves grows not more than six inches high, where the yellow star-shaped flowers appear on the spikes. It flourishes in bog conditions on the hills. It is more common in the north than in the south of the country.

Flowers July to August

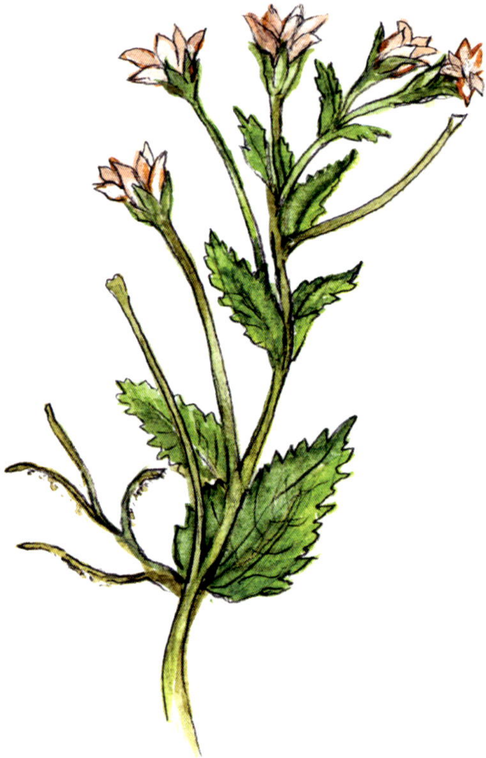

BROAD-LEAVED WILLOWHERB

Epilobium montanum *Family ONAGRACEAE*

One to two feet high, with short stemmed toothed leaves. Several together, the droopy headed buds, straighten when in flower – these are small with four pink petals. Widespread in woods and hedge banks.

Flowers June onwards

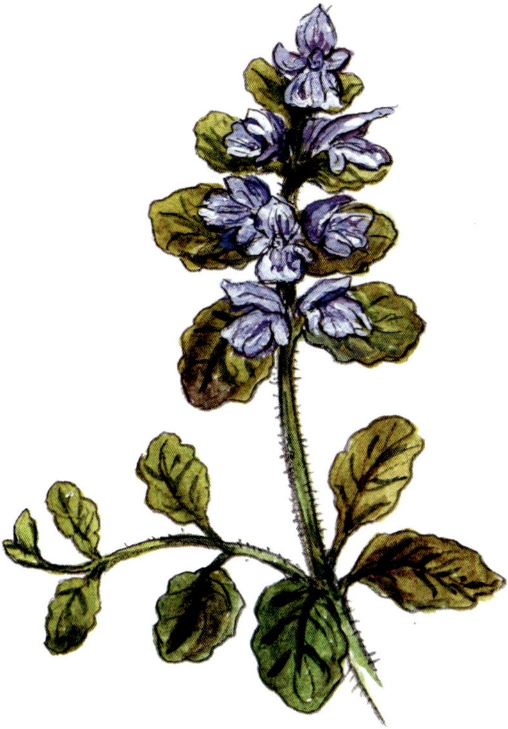

BUGLE

Ajuga reptans *Family LABIATAE*

This plant has a hairy stem and pairs of hairless leaves growing up the stalk. The powder-blue to pink or white flowers come in clusters among the leaves, ending in a spike.

Flowers April to June

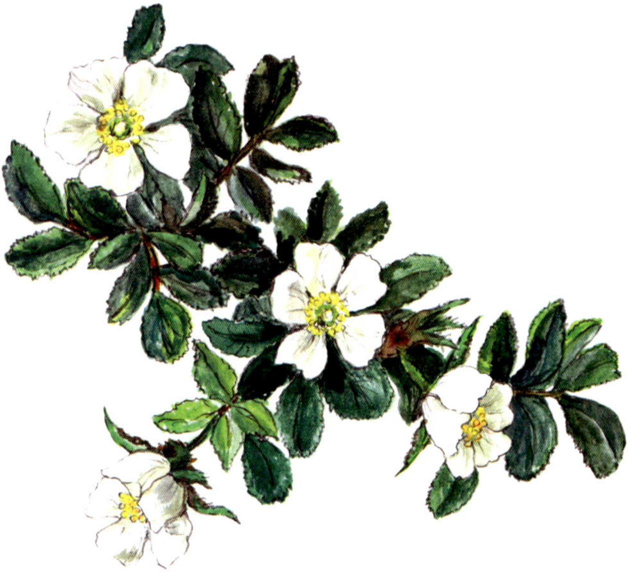

BURNET ROSE

Rosa pimpinellifolia *Family ROSACEAE*

Bushes of this rose appear on high limestone scree and must be very rare in Swaledale. It has fragrant creamy/white flowers, though sometimes slightly pink. The hips are purple/ black. It tends to hybridise with other roses which can cause confusion.

Flowers May to June.

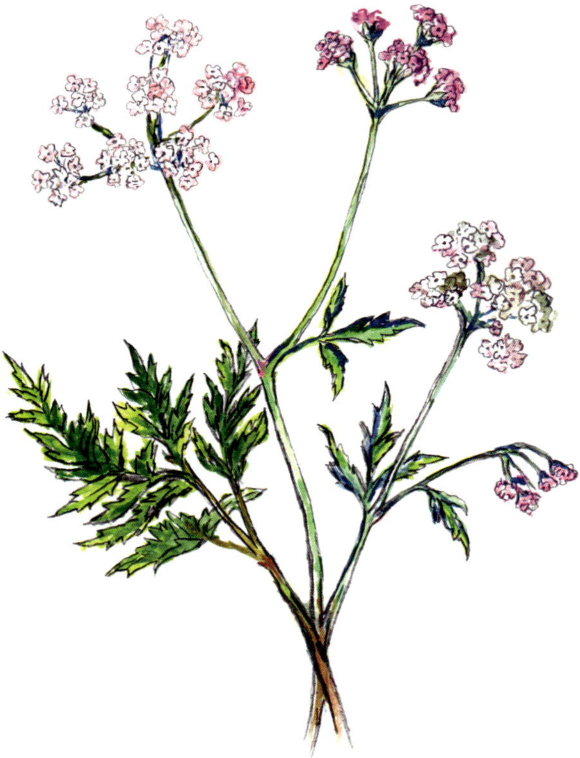

BURNET SAXIFRAGE

Pimpinella saxifraga *Family UMBELLIFERAE*

This plant is not a Burnet nor a Saxifrage. It is an Umbellifer. The lower leaves differ from the upper. The slightly hairy stems grow to two feet high. It grows in dry places on the edges of woodland or roadsides, managing to confuse us among all the other members of the parsley family.
Flowers June to August.

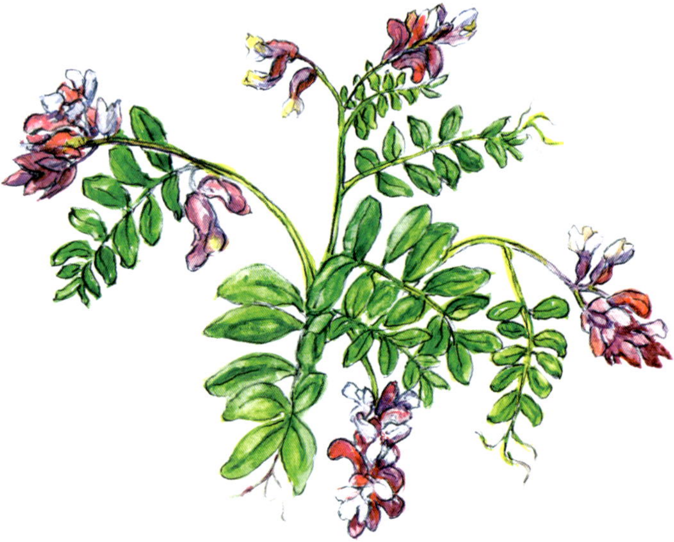

BUSH VETCH

Vicia sepium *Family LEGUMINOSAE*

This showy white and purple pea-shaped flower has branched tendrils at the end of slender stems of small leaves, which grow opposite each other. The plant clambers over other plants in hedges and bushy places.

Flowers April to September.

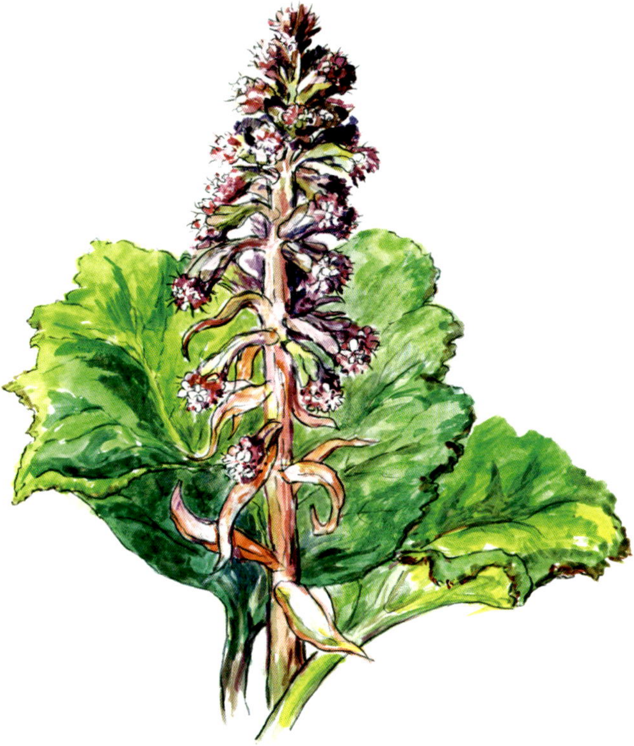

BUTTERBUR

Petasites hybridus *Family COMPOSITAE*

With huge leaves, greyish underneath with cottony hairs, this plant inhabits wet areas and banks. The flower heads are pale lilac green, and appear mainly before the large rhubarb-like foliage. Male and female flowers are on separate plants.

Flowers March to May.

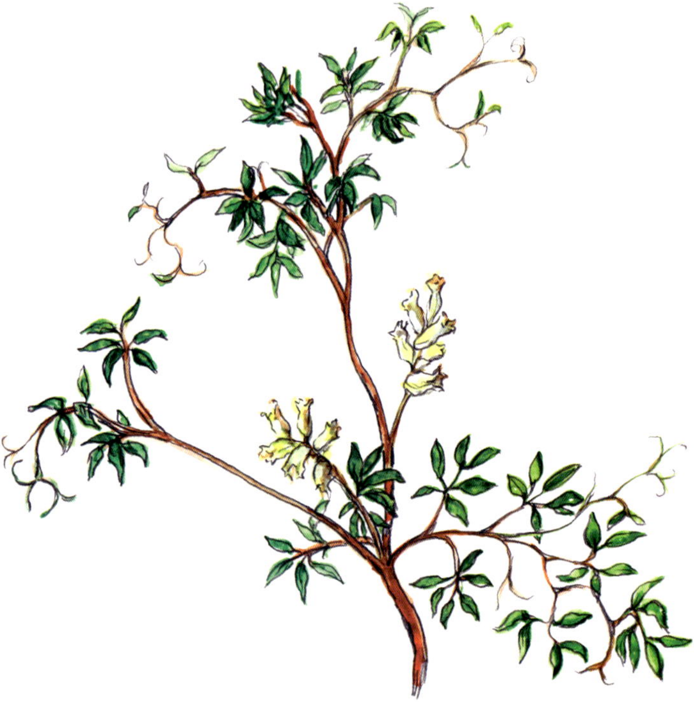

CLIMBING CORYDALIS

Corydalis claviculata *Family FUMARIACEAE*

This uncommon plant is an annual which grows in the woods and shady hedgerows clambering over other plants. It has small pale flowers spreading from a fine stem. It likes peaty soil.

Flowers June to September.

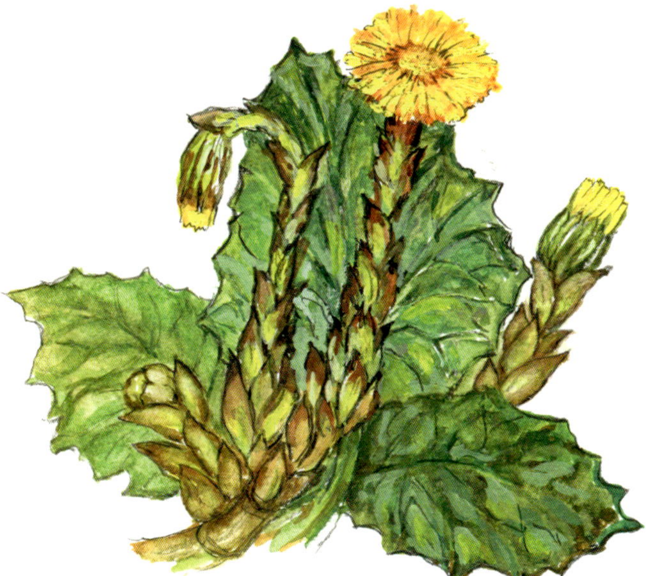

COLTSFOOT

Tussilago farfara *Family COMPOSITAE*

This yellow flower rises on a wooly, purplish stem which is covered closely by scaly leaflets, before the large leaves at its base appear. The leaves have white wooly hairs on their undersides. The name, *Tussis*, means cough in Latin, and the plant was once used to make a cough mixture.

Flowers February to April.

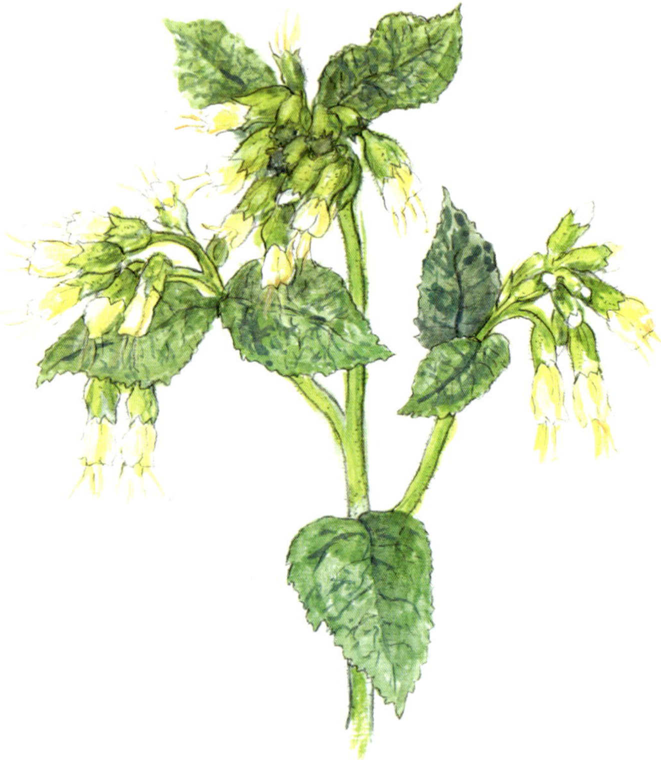

COMFREY

Symphytum officinale *Family BORAGINACEAE*

This flower can appear in various colours but seems to be white or cream most commonly in the dale. It favours damp places in ditches and hedgerows, in the valley bottom. Once the leaves were infused as a tea for the cure for chest infections, and its roots were made into a poultice for bruises and skin lesions.

Flowers May to September.

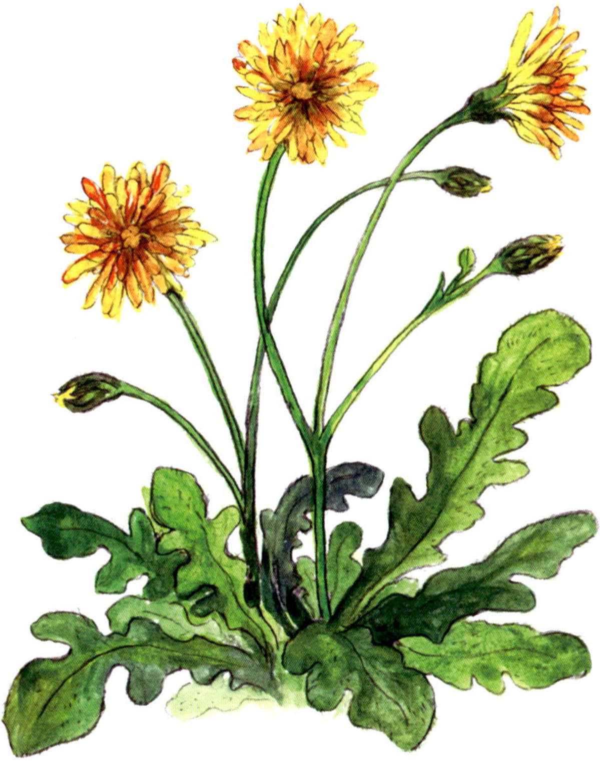

COMMON CATSEAR

Hypochaeris radicata *Family COMPOSITAE*

Abundant on dry grassy banks. It has solitary flowers on short branched stems.

Flowers June to September

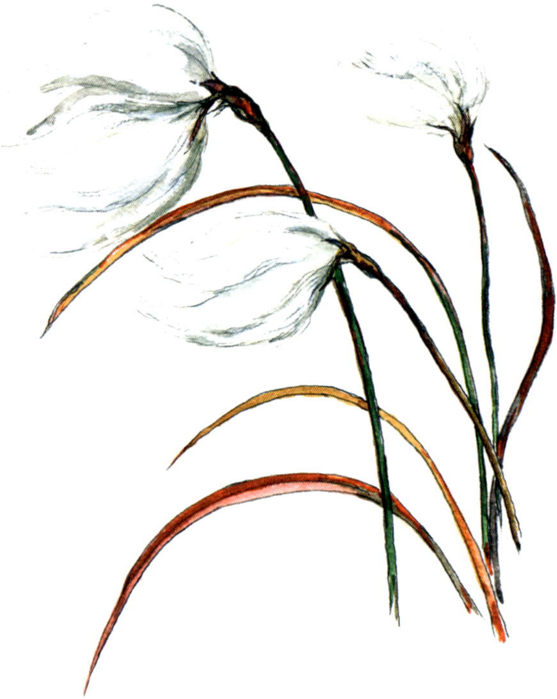

COMMON COTTON GRASS

Epiophorum augustifolium *Family CYPERACEAE*

It is the beautiful seed heads which catch the eye, not the rather insignificant little brown flowers. Patches of the white 'cotton' spread in the moorland, about ten to twelve inches high on grassy stems, and are an attractive sight when the heather is beginning to lose its colour.

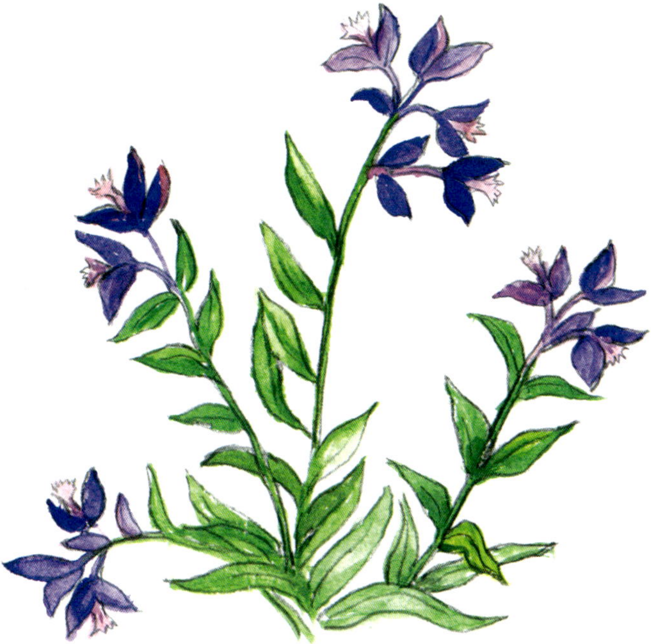

COMMON MILKWORT

Polygala vulgaris *Family POLYGALACEAE*

This delicate blue to purple little flower with touches of pink, grows in drier pastures and banks.

Flowers May to September.

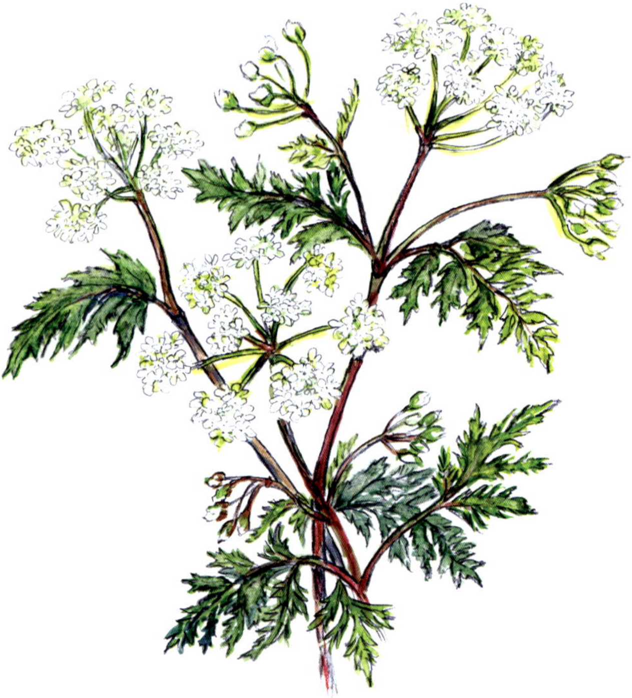

COW PARSLEY or Wild Chervil

Anthriscus sylvestris *Family UMBELLIFERAE*

This two to three foot umbellifer is one of the commonest growing along the roadsides in spring. The white flowers make a lacy, white froth, creating a background for other intruding colourful plants. It has broad dissected leaves of dark green, and hollow stems.

Flowers April to June.

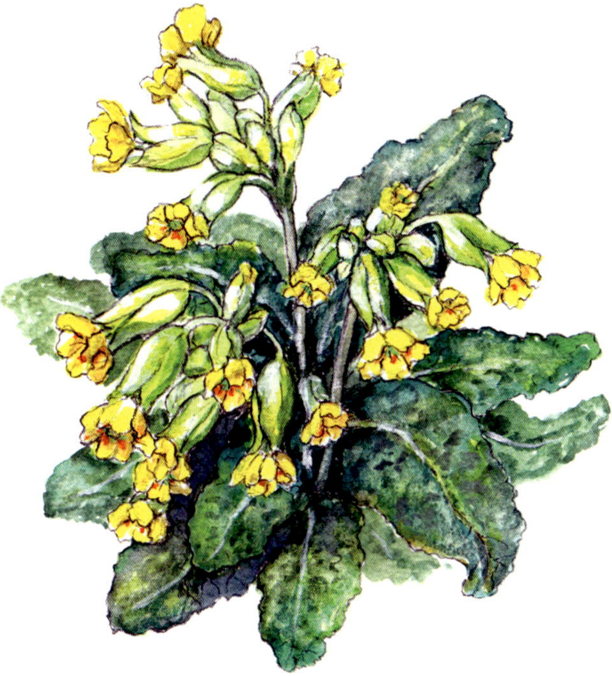

COWSLIP

Primula veris *Family PRIMULACEAE*

This pretty yellow flower is not as common in the dale as it is further south. However, clumps can be found in meadows and roadsides. It can be brewed as a tea where it is said to relieve insomnia, tension and headaches.

Flowers April to May.

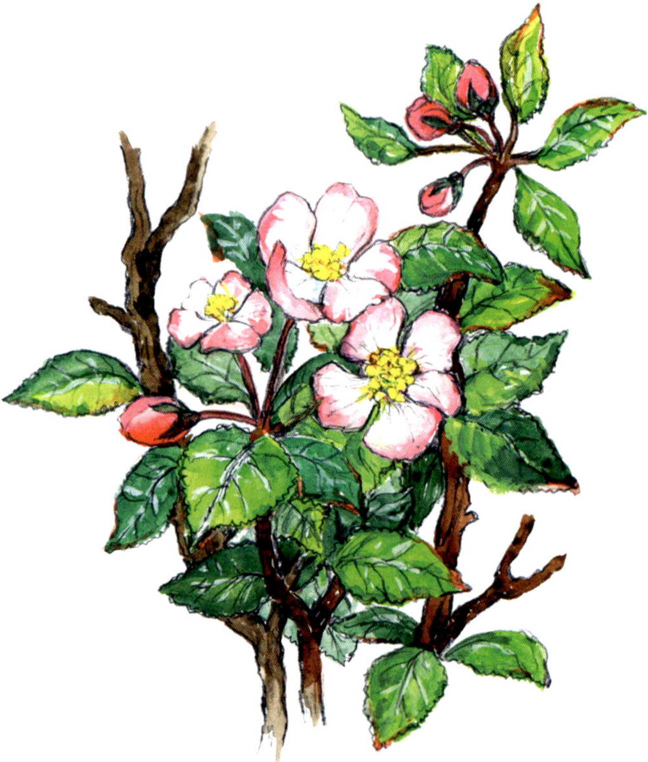

CRAB APPLE

Malus sylvestris *Family ROSACEAE*

This small tree appears, often solitary, in several places in the Swale valley, occasionally it has been used for hedging. Its prolific branches produce attractive white or pink flowers. The true crab apple has white blossom and small green fruit, whereas the wild apple has pink flowers and larger fruit.

Flowers May to June.

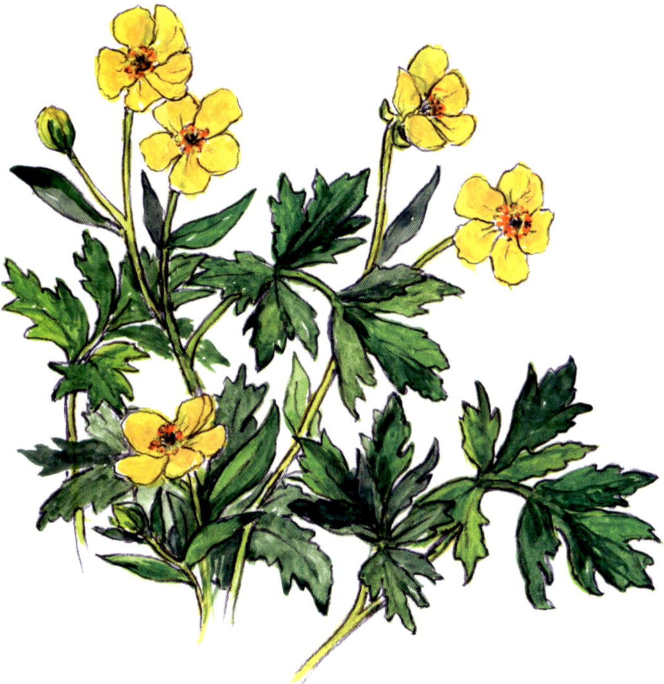

CREEPING BUTTERCUP

Ranunculus repens *Family RANUNCULACEAE*

An unpopular flower in gardens as it creeps on long shoots through grass, from where it roots to form a new plant. It loves lawns and makes a good yellow show in hayfield meadows.

Flowers May to September.

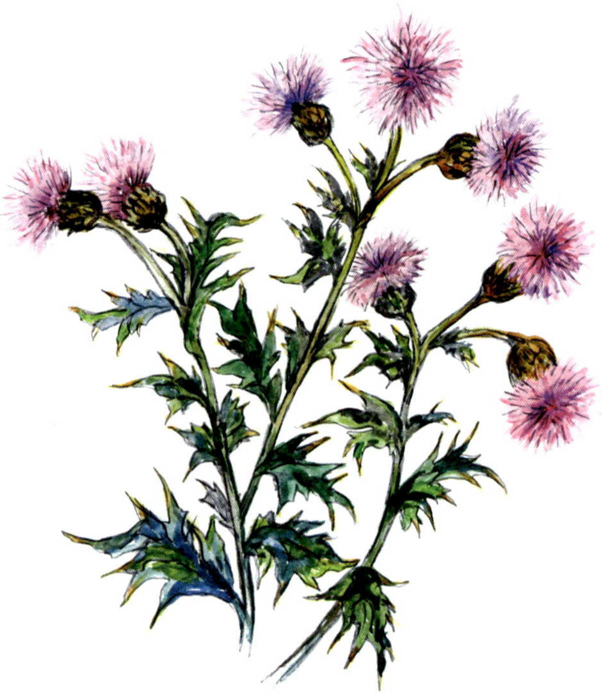

CREEPING THISTLE or COMMON THISTLE

Cirsium arvense *Family COMPOSITAE*

This plant can grow from one to three foot, with very spiky leaves. It is in common grassy areas from the valley to the hillsides. Male and female plants are separate, the roots spread and shoot up stems.

Flowers July to September.

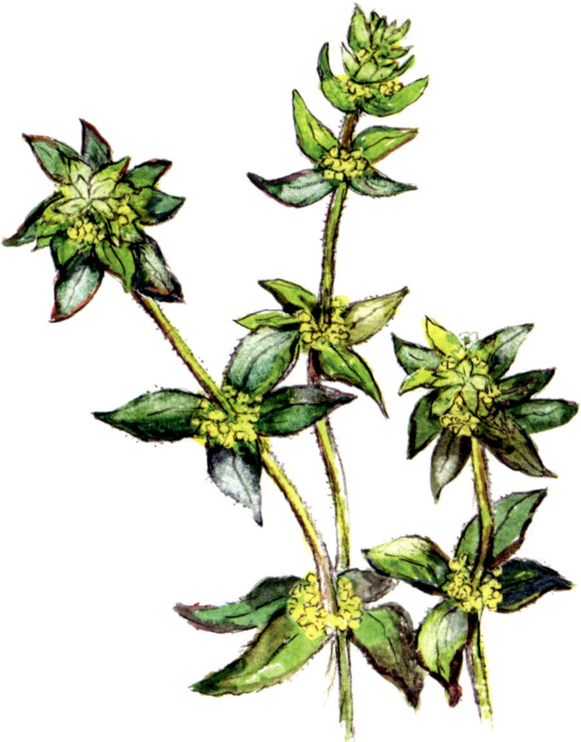

CROSSWORT

Galium cruciata *Family RUBIACEAE*

This erect plant has small yellow flowers nestling closely to the stem in a cross of four little leaves. It is a hairy plant with a sweet smell, and grows most happily on grassland on limestone slopes.

Flowers May to July.

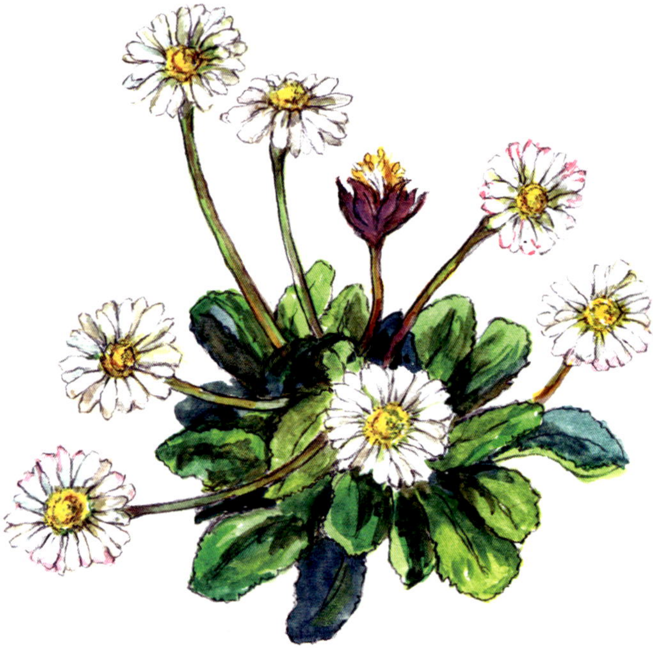

DAISY

Bellis perennis *Family COMPOSITAE*

This well known little white flower with occasional pink on the tip of its petals, grows in fields, lawns and banks on the lower slopes of the dale.

Flowers March to October.

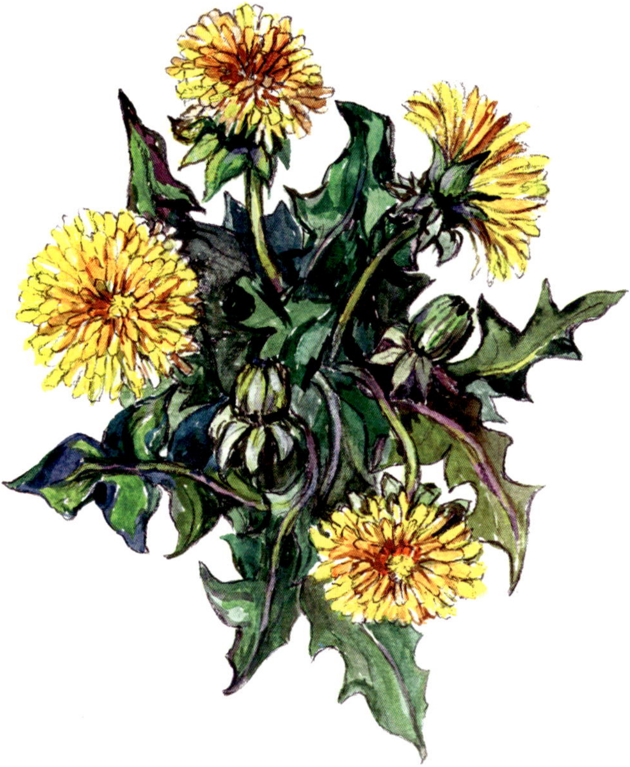

DANDELION

Taraxacum officinale *Family COMPOSITAE*

This common bright yellow flower can make a brilliant show along the Dale's roadsides and waste ground.

Flowers March to October.

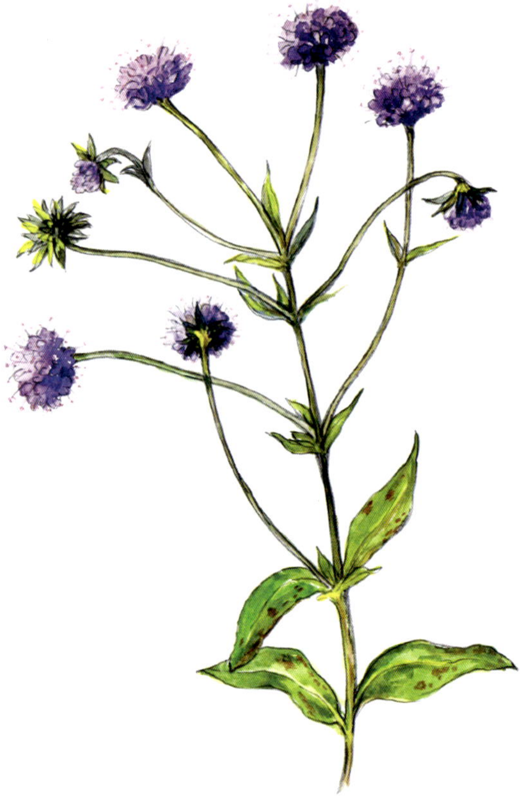

DEVIL'S BIT SCABIOUS

Succisa pratensis *Family DIPSACACEAE*

A rounded, blue/mauve flower, at the end of a long stem, is found in hedgerows and on banks where it favours dampness. The short rootstock is believed to have been bitten off by the devil.

Flowers July to October.

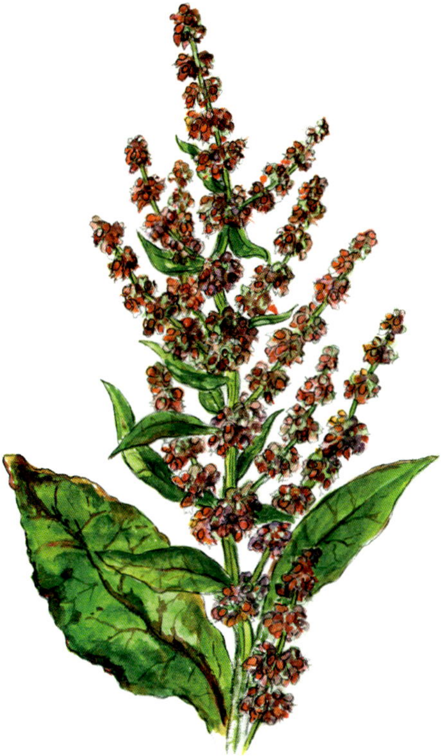

DOCK (BROAD-LEAVED)

Rumex obtusifolius *Family POLYGONACEAE*

A common Dock has leafy flower stems. The pinkish flowers rise up the stem in little clumps. The base leaves are slightly heart shaped. It grows in hedges and ditches, particularly around farms. It is always handy where there are nettles as the leaves are said to relieve stings.

Flowers May to June.

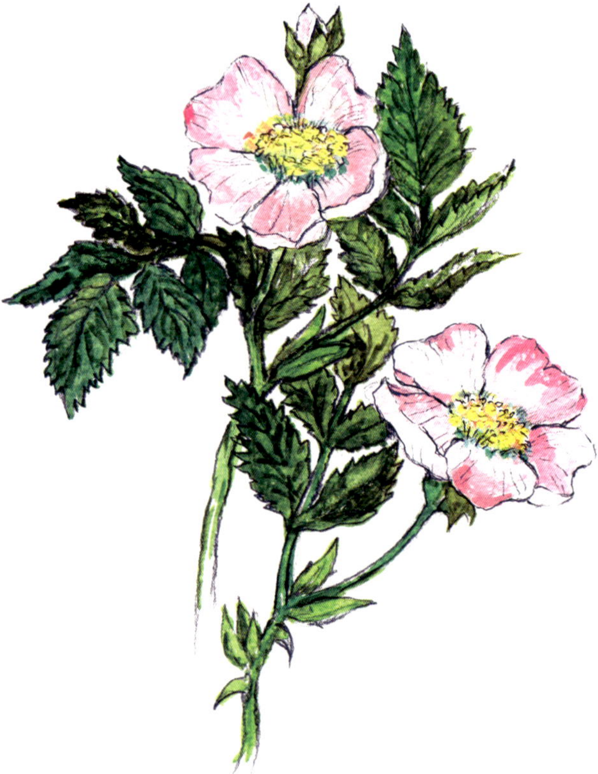

DOG ROSE

Rosa canina *Family ROSACEAE*

The most common, but variable of the wild roses. It has the largest flowers of pale pink, to white with a fragrant scent. It has arching stems and egg-shaped hips.

Flowers June to July.

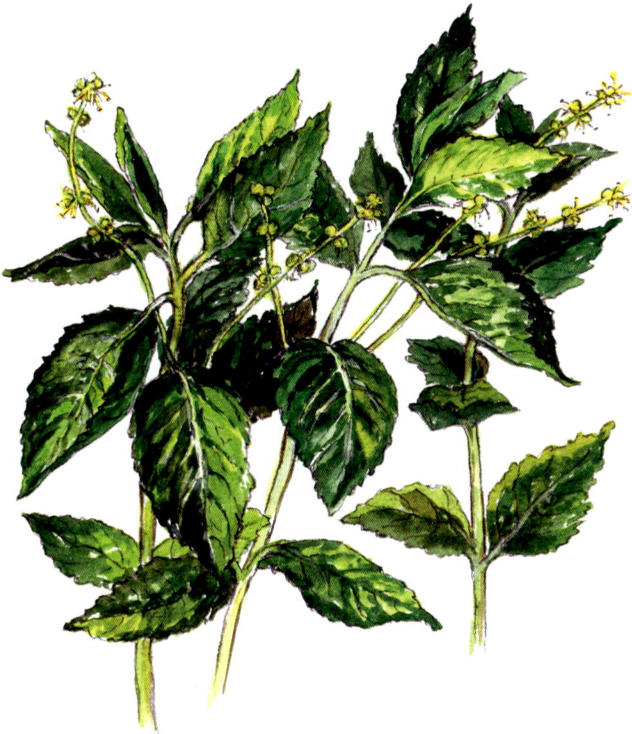

DOGS MERCURY

Mercurialis perennis *Family EUPHORBIACEAE*

This plant covers the floor of woods in the valley. It can be found among shady rocks, and uncommonly thrives in beech woods. It has insignificant little white flowers, and male and females are on different plants. The pollen is carried by the wind. As the name suggests, this plant is poisonous.

Flowers April to May.

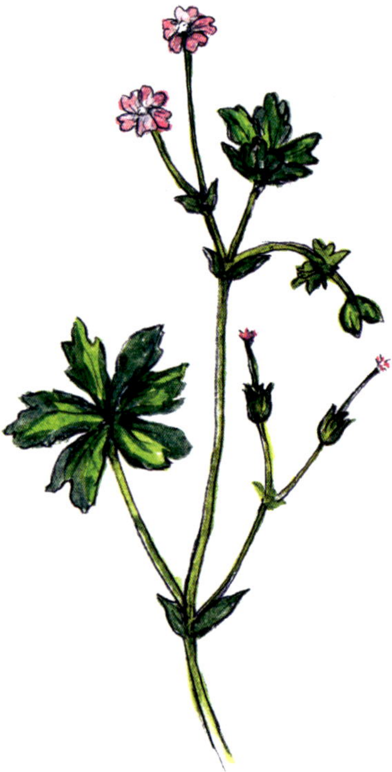

DOVE'S FOOT CRANESBILL

Geranium molle *Family GERANIACEAE*

A very common annual. It has branched, spreading stems with red to purple and white little flowers. It is covered with white hairs. It favours dryish, grassy paces.

Flowers April to September.

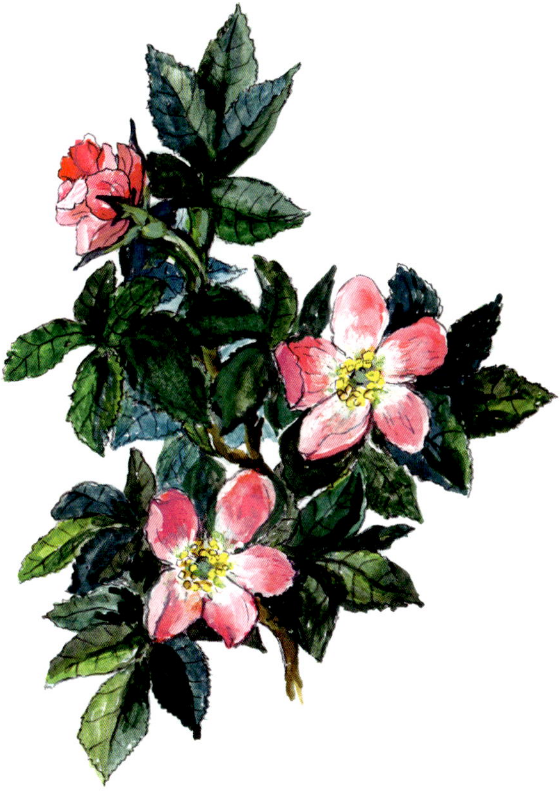

DOWNY ROSE

Rosa tomentosa *Family ROSACEAE*

This densely downy plant has deep pink flowers and straight spines, and is particularly common in northern hedgerows.

Flowers from June to July.

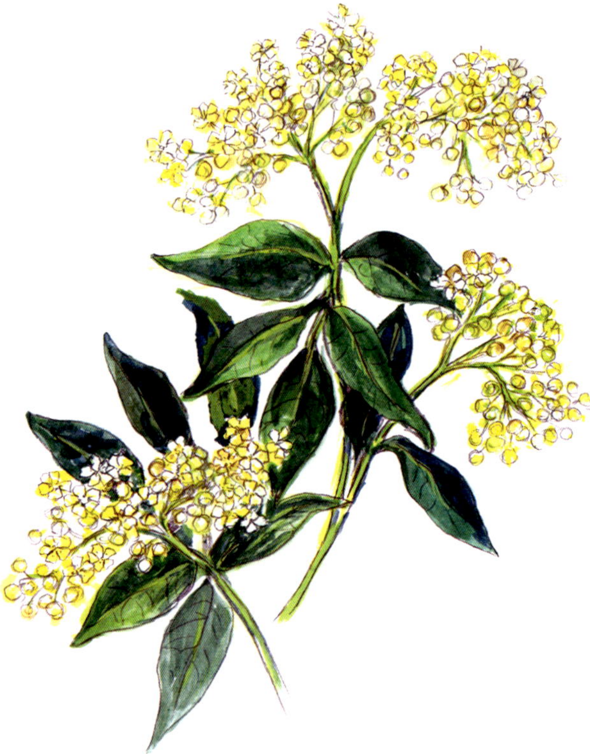

ELDER

Sambucus nigra *Family CAPRIFOLIACEAE*

This is a shrub or small tree which grows in hedges and scattered on the hillsides throughout the dales. It has small white flowers which form a flat head about five to six inches across. It has dark purple to black berries. Both the flowers and the fruit make delicious cordials and wines.

Flowers June to July.

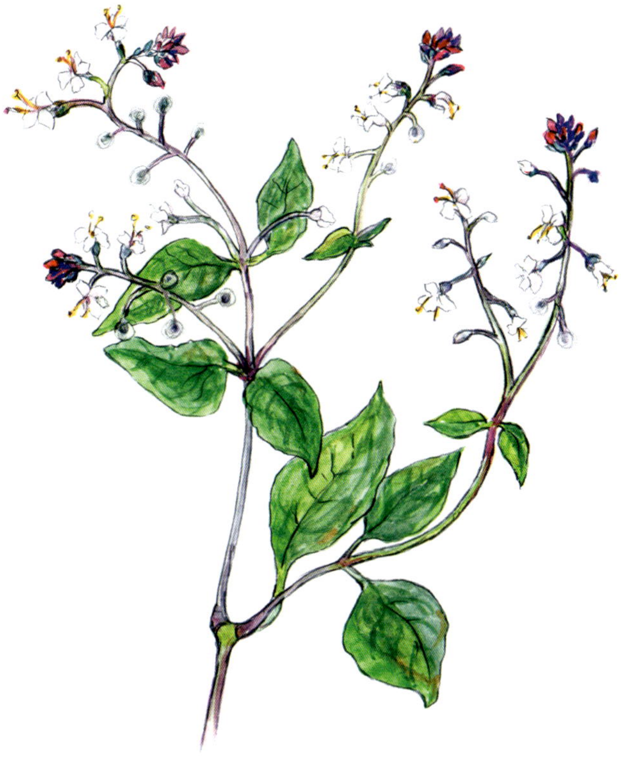

ENCHANTER'S NIGHTSHADE

Circaea lutetiana *Family ONAGRACEAE*

This is a slightly hairy perennial with small white flowers, which grows from one to two feet high in woodlands and shady places, in the valley bottom. Its fruits are covered in hooked hairs. It is no relation of other nightshades.

Flowers June to August.

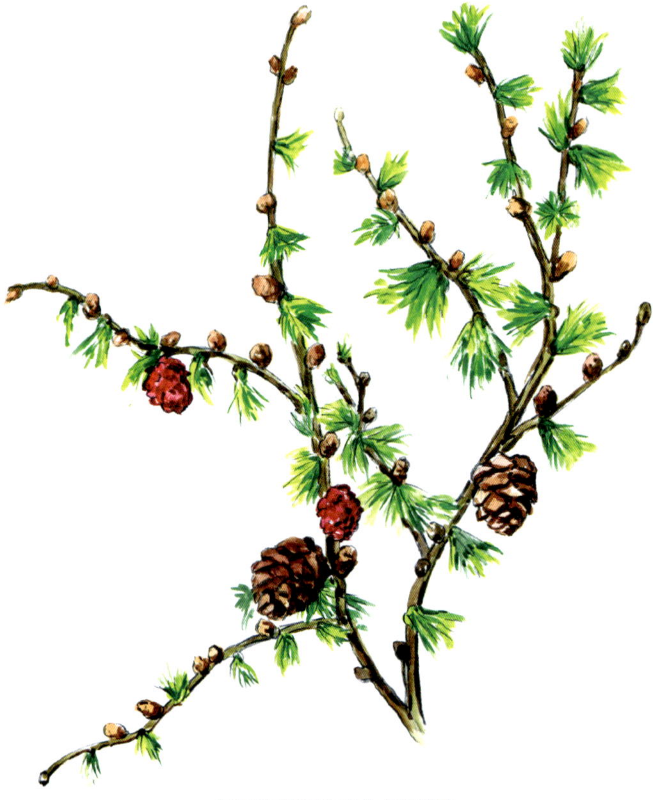

EUROPEAN LARCH

Larix decidua *Family PINACEAE*

This tree is usually planted. It loses its needle-like spines in winter when the small oval cones are visible. It has small red flowers clinging to its branches. The end branches sometimes droop downwards.

Flowers May to June.

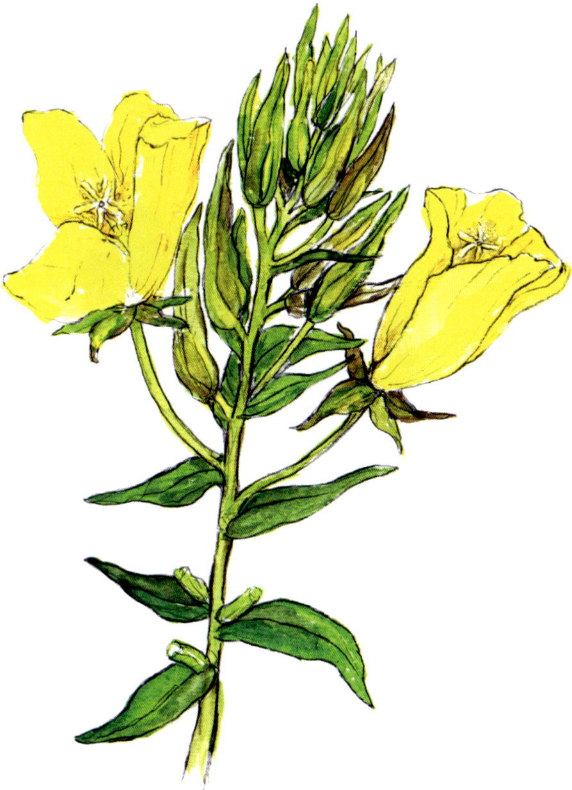

EVENING PRIMROSE

Oenothera biennis *Family ONAGRACEAE*

This large yellow flower has possibly escaped from gardens. It can be found on the outskirts of Richmond making a splash of colour in damp ditches.

Flowers June to September.

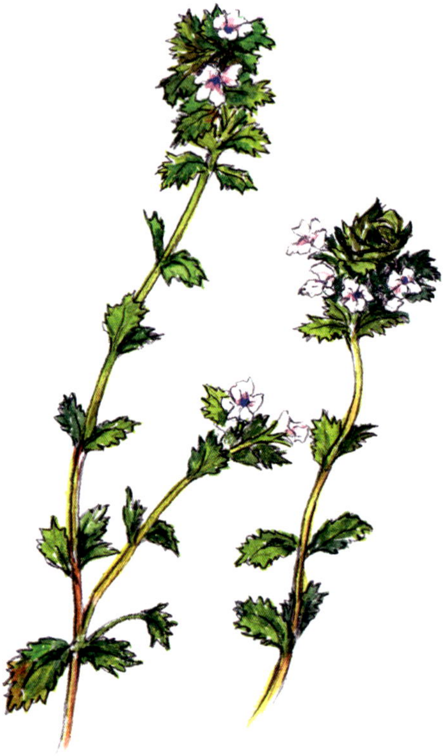

EYEBRIGHT

Euphrasia officinalis *Family SCROPHULARIACEAE*

This very pretty little flower appears on leafy stems from a dark green and hairy low plant. The little white flowers are often tinged with purple and have a yellow spot on the lower lip. At one time it was thought to help sore eyes and nasal catarrh. It can be found in grassy places throughout the dales.

Flowers June to September.

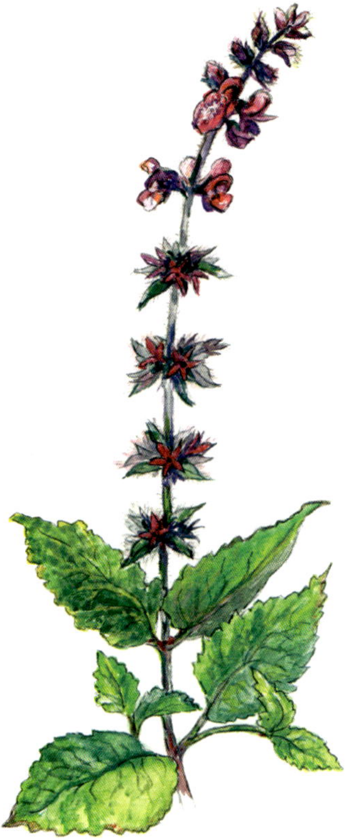

FIELD WOUNDWORT

Stachys arvensis *Family LABIATAE*

Twelve inches high, this claret-coloured flowers appear close to leaves up the stem. It grows for preference where ground has been disturbed in hedges and ditches in the valley.

Flowers from April.

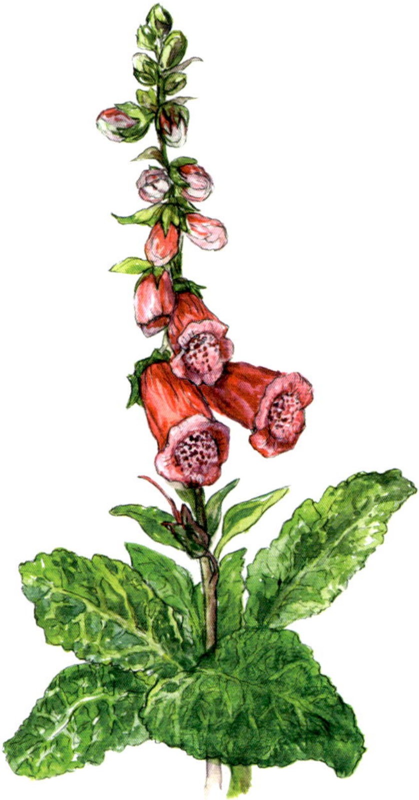

FOXGLOVE

Digitalis purpurea *Family SCROPHULARIACEAE*

This colourful pink flower, whose spikes bring a welcome splash of colour to the hillsides and woods, where it prefers dry soil. It self-seeds prolifically. Although poisonous it is known for its continued medical qualities.

Flowers July to September.

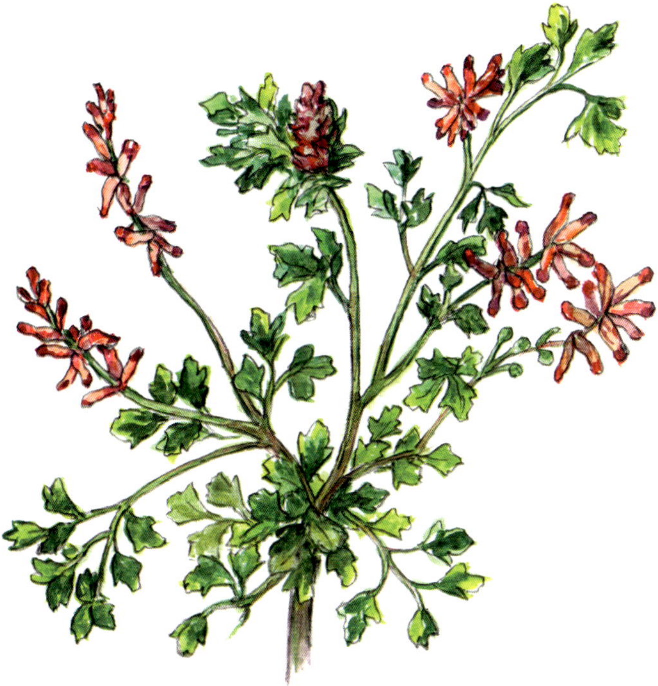

FUMITORY

Fumaria officinalis *Family FUMARIACEAE*

In various shades of pink and purple, often tipped with maroon,
This flower grows on cultivated ground, gardens and banks.

Flowers May to August.

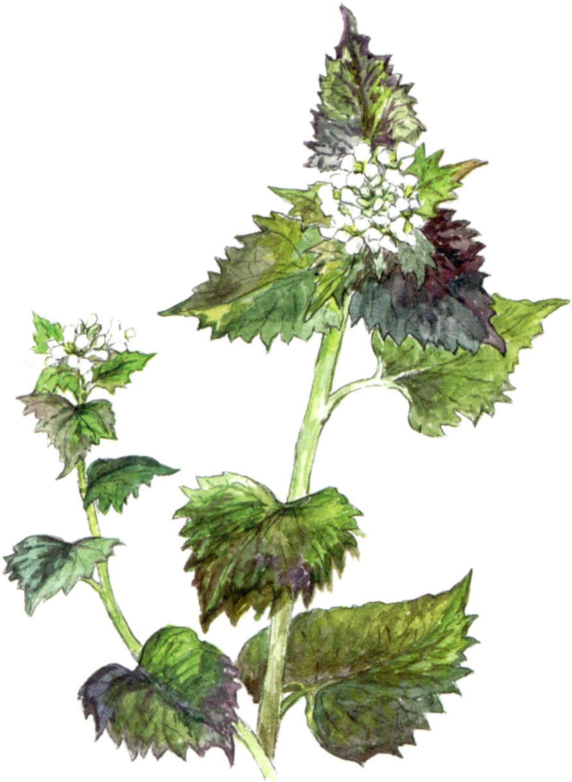

GARLIC MUSTARD or Jack-by-the-Hedge

Alliaria petiolata *Family CRUCIFERAE*

A common spring biennial, it can grow to three feet high. It has fresh green, stalked, heart-shaped and toothed leaves, with small white flowers. When crushed it smells of garlic. It grows in hedgerows and woods.

Flowers April to June.

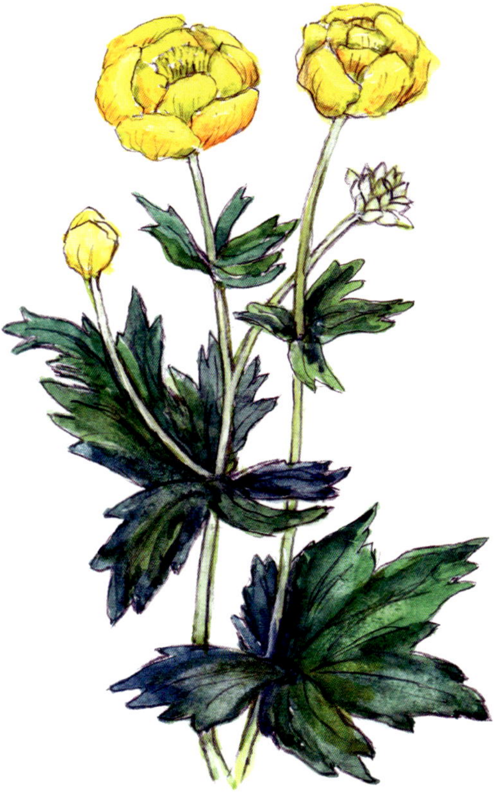

GLOBE FLOWER

Trollius europaeus *Family RANUNCULACEAE*

Unlike buttercups, the globe flower has rounded, yellow flowers, which grow up to an inch across, without green sepals. These flowers are not very common, but grow abundantly in some damp pastures in the Dales. They mostly grow in the north of the country.

Flowers May to August.

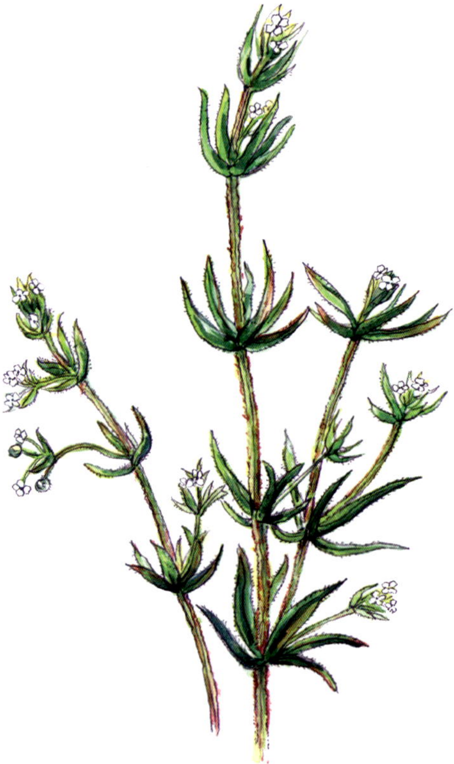

GOOSEGRASS (or Cleavers)

Galium aparine *Family RUBIACEAE*

This plant is well known for clinging onto one's clothing if one gets too close. It will climb over bushes and other plants to four or five feet, hanging on by tiny down-turned hooks. The hardly visible flowers are white and come in tiny clusters. The habitat is widespread in hedgerows and wasteland on the lower slopes and valleys.

Flowers June to August.

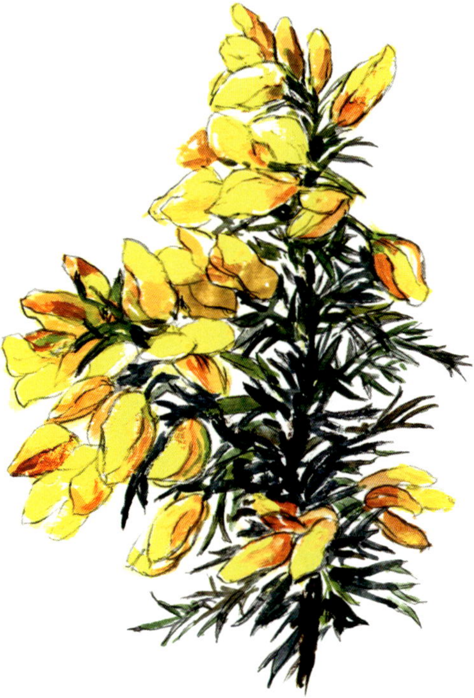

GORSE or Furze or Whin

Ulex europaeus *Family LEGUMINOSAE*

A densely spiky shrub which grows on hillsides in an evergreen mass. It is said to always have one in flower all the year, and that "kissing is out of season when gorse is out of bloom." The deep yellow pea-shaped flower, has a strong buttery/almond scent. It is uncommon in Swaledale.

Flowers April to June.

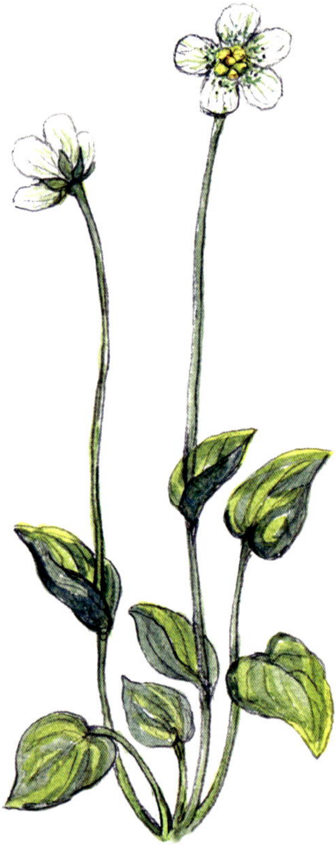

GRASS OF PARNASSUS

Parnassia palustris *Family PARNASSIACEAE*

A single white, five petalled flower with green veins appears on a straight, leafless stalk. It has heart-shaped leaves which cling to the lower stalk. It likes marshy places and spring flushes. It is a rare and beautiful plant.

Flowers July to September.

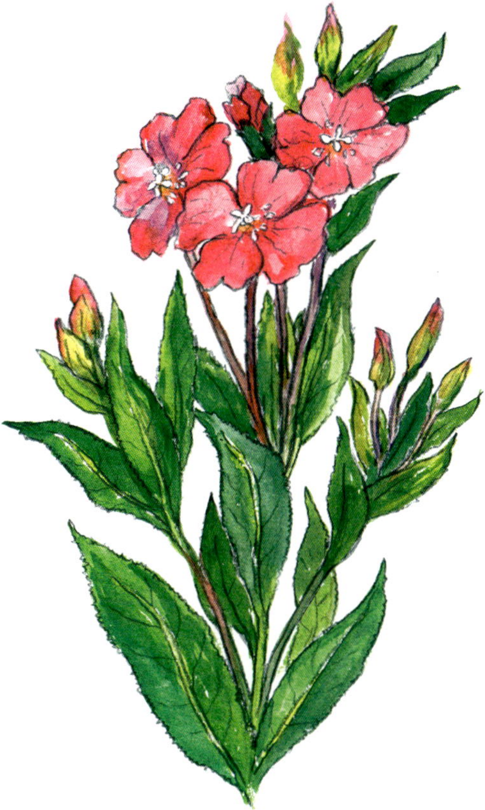

GREAT WILLOWHERB

Epilobium hirsutum *Family ONAGRACEAE*

The tallest of the willow herbs often reaching four foot high and more. It thrives on river banks and bogs, with quite showy flowers of four pink petals surrounded by toothy leaves.

Flowers July to August.

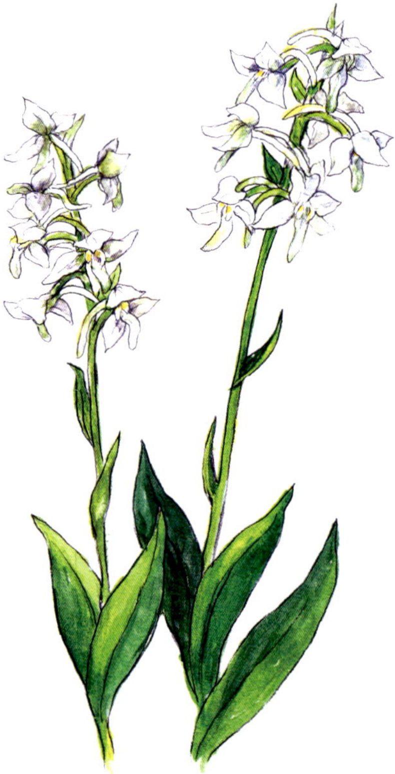

GREATER BUTTERFLY ORCHID

Platanthera chlorantha *Family ORCHIDACEAE*

One of the most attractive orchids can only be found flourishing in a few pastures in the dale. This delicate greenish white flower appears rather later than some other orchids, and because of its unique colour cannot be confused with the more colourful varieties.

Flowers June to July.

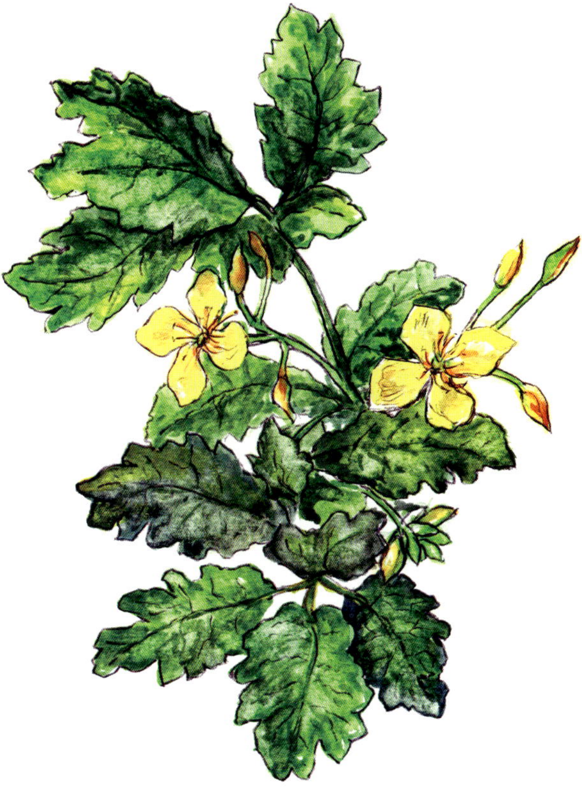

GREATER CELANDINE

Chelidonium majus *Family MECANOPSIS*

This bushy plant grows to about eighteen inches high. It has an insignificant yellow flower compared to the bright lesser celandine. It grows in fields and gardens, liking to be near buildings and is said to be poisonous to animals. It has an orange juice when the stem is crushed.

Flowers May to September.

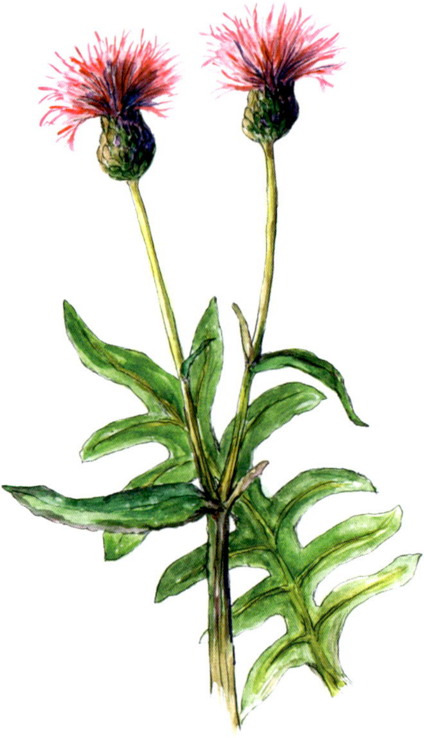

GREATER KNAPWEED

Centaurea scabiosa *Family COMPOSITAE*

It is much larger than the common Lesser Knapweed and is rare in the north. It is similar in appearance, with an almost thistle-like purple flower, however unlike the thistle family, it has no prickly spikes. It has large green leaves and lives in grassy places on the hillsides.

Flowers July to September.

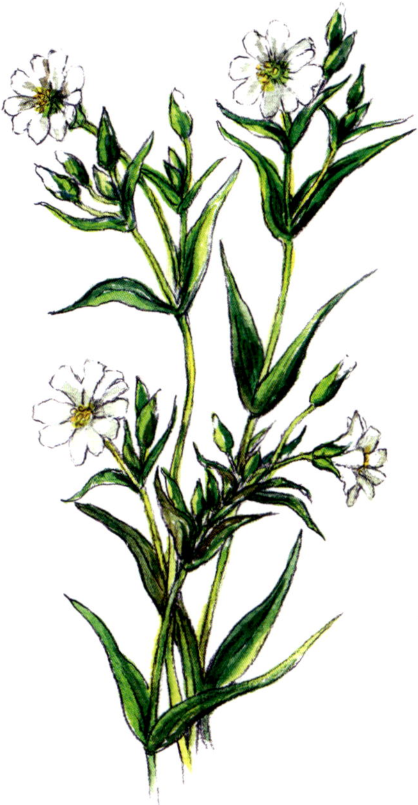

GREATER STITCHWORT

Stellaria holostea *Family CARYOPHYLLACEAE*

This pretty white flower grows from a straggly plant, sometimes two feet high, in woods and hedges.

Flowers April to June.

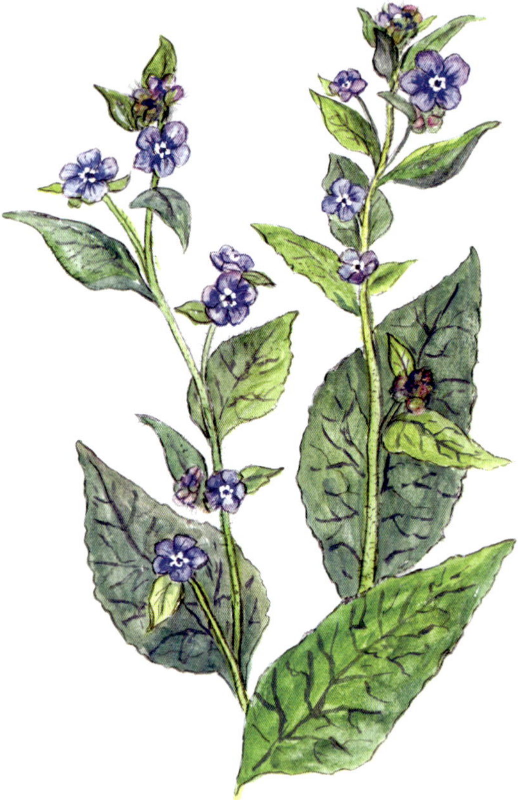

GREEN ALKANET

Pentaglottis sempervirens *Family BORAGINACEAE*

This hairy plant grows from one to two feet tall. It has bright blue flowers with a white 'eye' and five petals. It grows in hedges and woods and is probably a garden escape.

Flowers May to August.

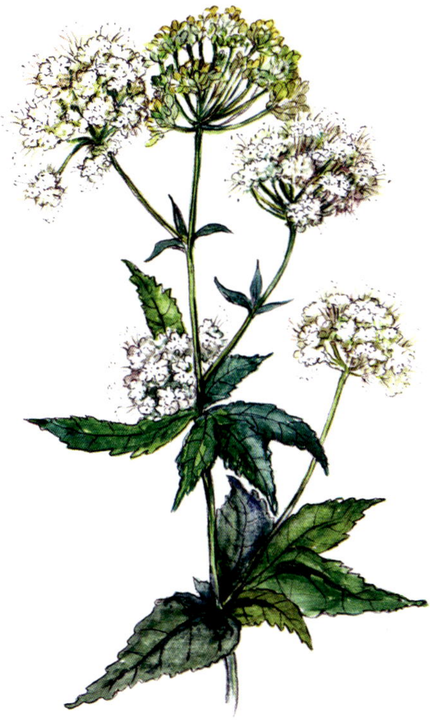

GROUND ELDER

Aegopodium podagraria *Family UMBELLIFERAE*

Gardeners hate this intrusive weed, which spreads from creeping rhizomes. This white to pink flower is said to have been introduced by the Romans who used the leaves as a vegetable. It flourishes along the dale's roadsides, and is a scurge to gardeners with a tangle of roots which are almost impossible to remove.

Flowers March to June.

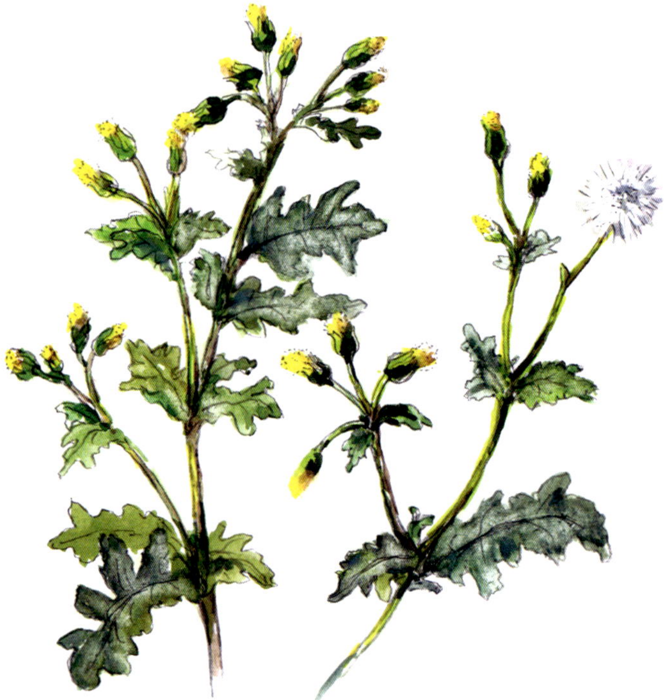

GROUNDSEL

Senecio vulgaris *Family COMPOSITAE*

This common garden weed (much favoured by buderigars) grows on waste ground and vegetable patches. It has a small yellow flower and fluffy white seed heads.

Flowers March to November.

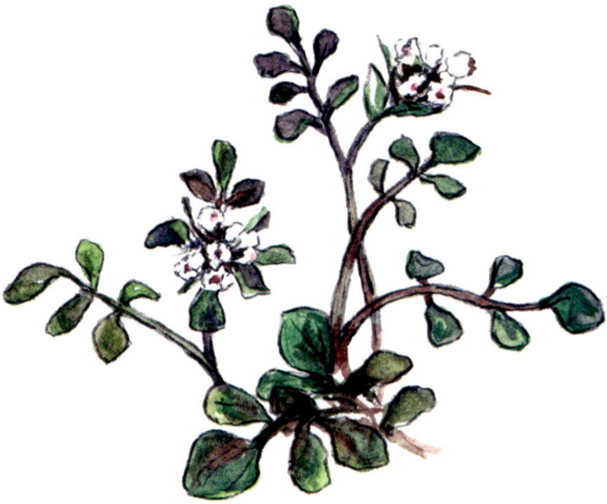

HAIRY BITTERCRESS

Cardamine hirsuta *Family CRUCIFERAE*

This is a common garden weed with small white flowers and long upright seed heads which extend above the flowers. It has small leaves along central stems and the main stalk grows from a rosette of leaves at ground level.

Flowers March to September.

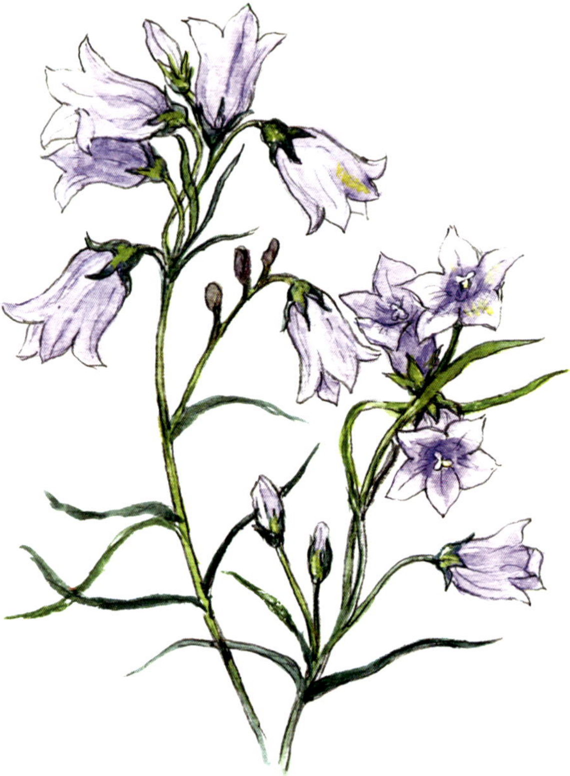

HAREBELL or Bluebell of Scotland

Campanula rotundifolia *Family CAMPANULACEAE*

In bright contrast to the green grass on the hillsides this fragile bell-shaped flower can be found quite commonly. The flower stems rise from narrow leaves which cling to the main stems.

Flowers July to September.

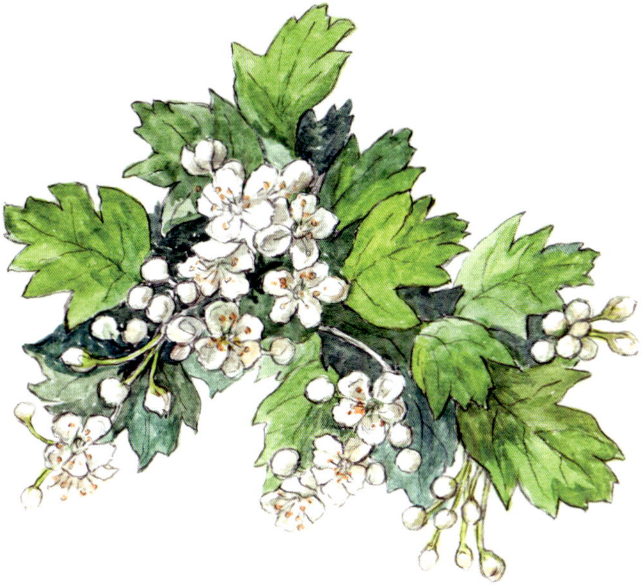

HAWTHORN

Crataegus monogyna *Family ROSACEAE*

A very common shrub, or small tree. It is found along roads and hedges, and frequently alone on the high hills. This thorny deciduous shrub is often found with twisted trunk in the remains of field hedges. It has white flowers (occasionally pink) which flower loosely together among the deeply lobed, dark green leaves. It bears a mass of dark red berries in the autumn, said to be forecasters of a hard winter!

Flowers May to June.

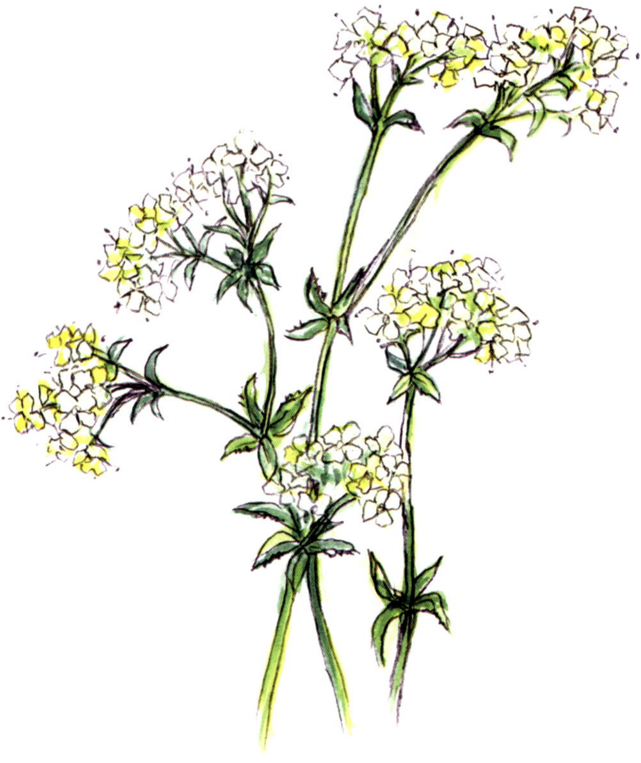

HEATH BEDSTRAW

Galium saxatile *Family RUBIACEAE*

This low, matted plant, has short whorls of small pointed leaves along its stems. The little white flowers cluster together along the stems on short stalks. this plant likes acid soil and is common throughout the district.

Flowers June to August.

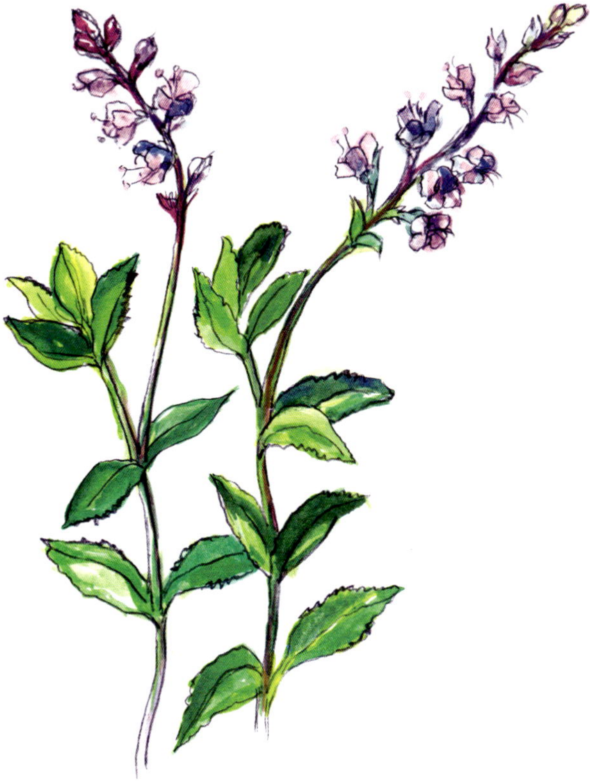

HEATH SPEEDWELL

Veronica officinalis *Family SCROPHULARIACEAE*

This plant grows in dry pastures and on roadside verges. It has lilac flowers on stalked spikes rising from coupled leaves.

Flowers June to September.

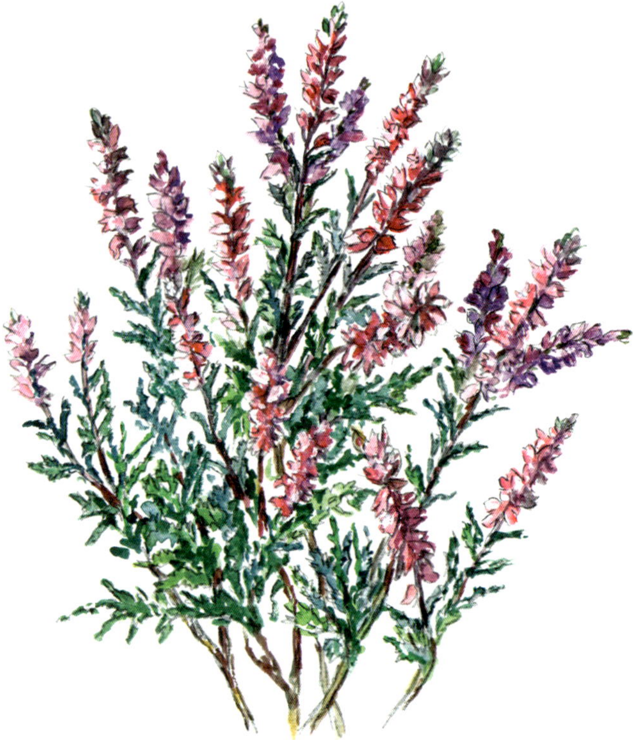

HEATHER

Calluna vulgaris *Family ERICACEAE*

Typical of the dales moorlands, this small shrub with a purple flower carpets the high hills in late summer. In winter it is regularly burnt in alternate patches, to promote growth of the young green shoots eaten by the grouse. The dark green, rough little leaves turn to deep brown and almost black as the winter closes in.

Flowers August to September.

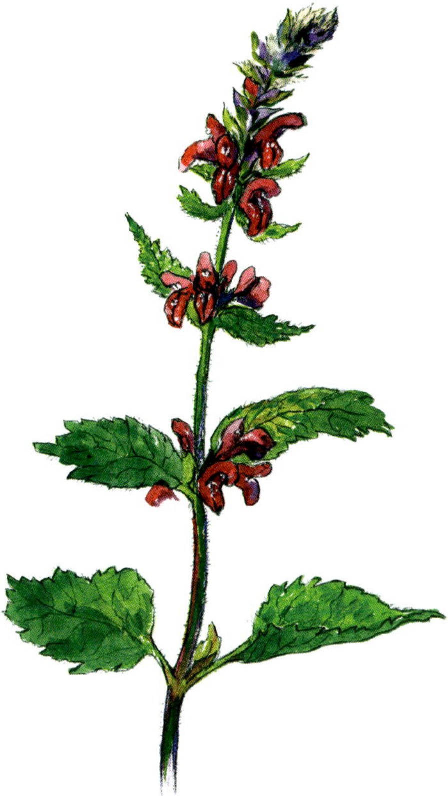

HEDGE WOUNDWORT

Stachys sylvatica *Family LABIATAE*

This plant is a hairy dark green perennial, which grows in hedges to about eighteen inches high. The dark purple flower grows up the stem to a spike, with small leaves at each base. It has a very pungent smell and is popular with bees.

Flowers June to August.

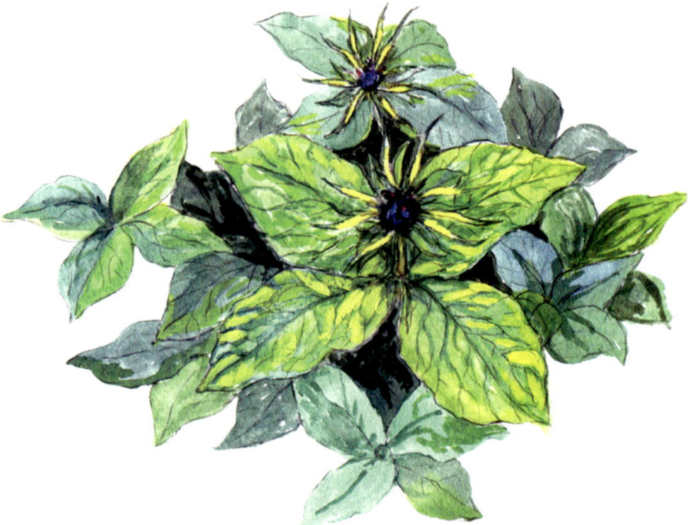

HERB PARIS

Parisquadrifolia *Family LILIACEAE*

A leafy green plant which grows under trees and in woodland where the soil is damp and alkaline. Surrounded by four leaves is the strangely shaped green and yellow flower. In the centre is a purple/black coloured berry which is poisonous. It is rare in Swaledale.

Flowers May to June.

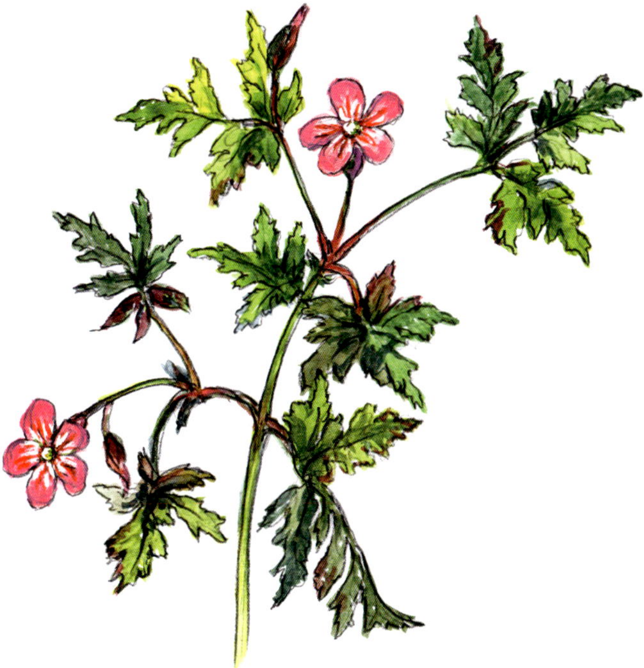

HERB ROBERT

Geranium robertianum *Family GERANIACEAE*

A rather hairy plant with half an inch pink flowers at the end of slender stalks. It has a strong smell, and fern-like triangular leaves. It grows in shady places, on stony ground and on walls.

Flowers May to September.

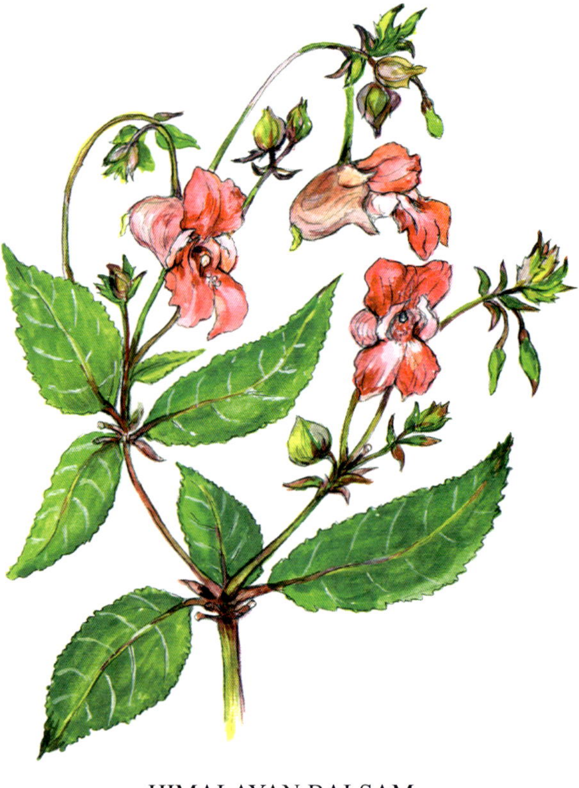

HIMALAYAN BALSAM

Impatiens glandulifera *Family BALSAMINACEAE*

An invasive newcomer, presumably escaped from gardens, this rather spectacular red/pink flower is spreading happily in damp hedgerows and is becoming dominant on river banks. In Swaledale, so far, it remains near Richmond. It grows up to three feet tall.

Flowers June to October.

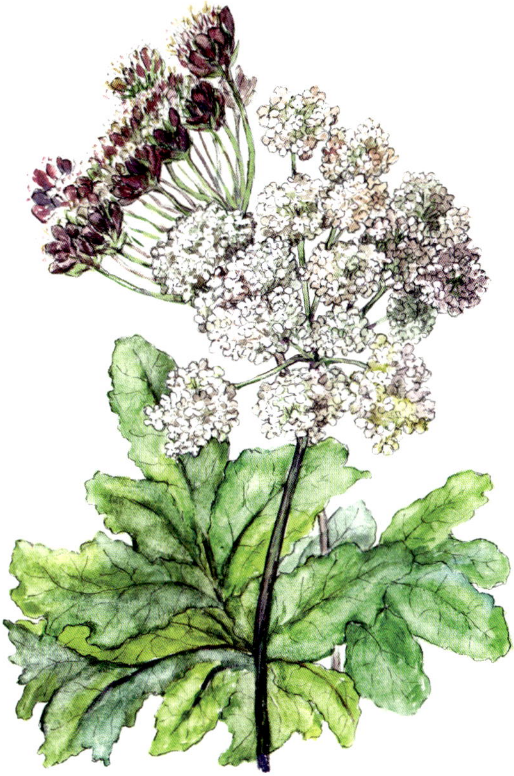

HOGWEED

Heracleum sphondylium *Family UMBELLIFERAE*

A tall plant reaching over three feet or more. The hollow stem has bristly hairs and the flowers are pinkish or white with five petals. The pig-like smell of the flowers gives the plant its name. It is common in hedges and meadows.

Flowers June to October.

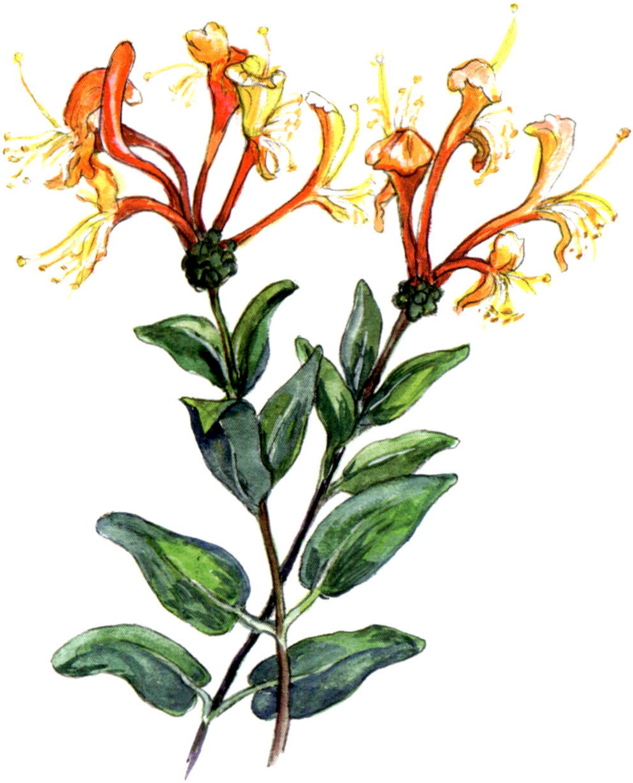

HONEYSUCKLE or Woodbine.
Lonicera periclymenum *Family CAPRIFOLIACEAE*

The honeysuckle climbs through hedgerows and shrubs in woodland. It is very sweet scented and attracts insects and moths in the evenings which pollinate the flowers.

Flowers June to September.

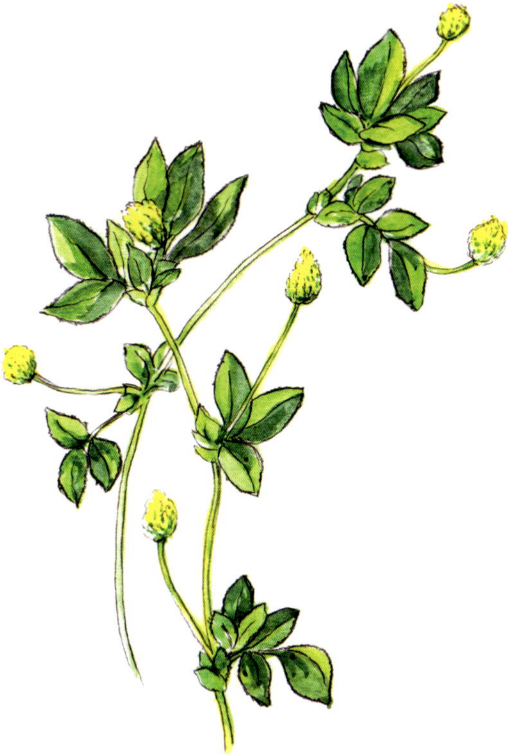

HOP TREFOIL

Trifolium compestre *Family LEGUMINOSAE*

This little plant's three leaves fan out at the base of each stem. The slender flower stem rises to hold the global head of tiny yellow flowers. It likes grassy places, on lower slopes.

Flowers May onwards.

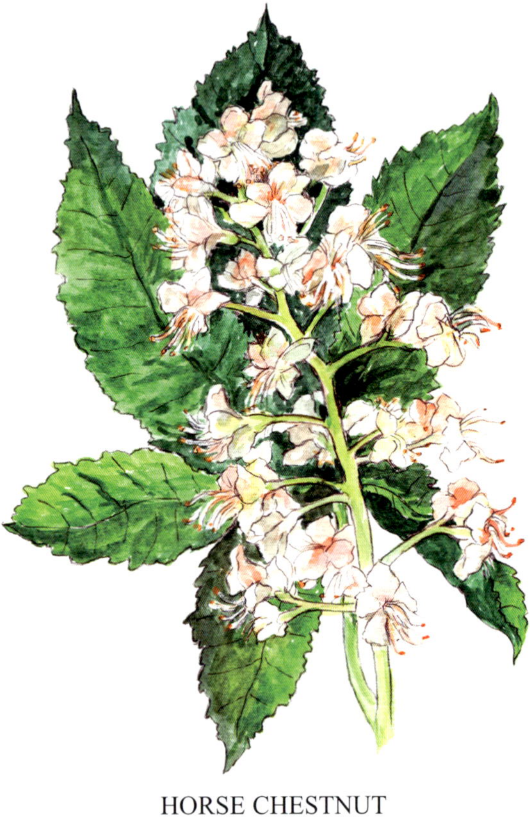

HORSE CHESTNUT

Aesculus hippocastanum *Family HIPPOCASTANACEAE*

Most likely to be found associated with houses, or along entrance driveways, this fine large tree has erect flower heads of white and pink, and the prickly seed enclosing a shiny 'conker', well known to children. It is not related to the Sweet Chestnut.

Flowers May to June.

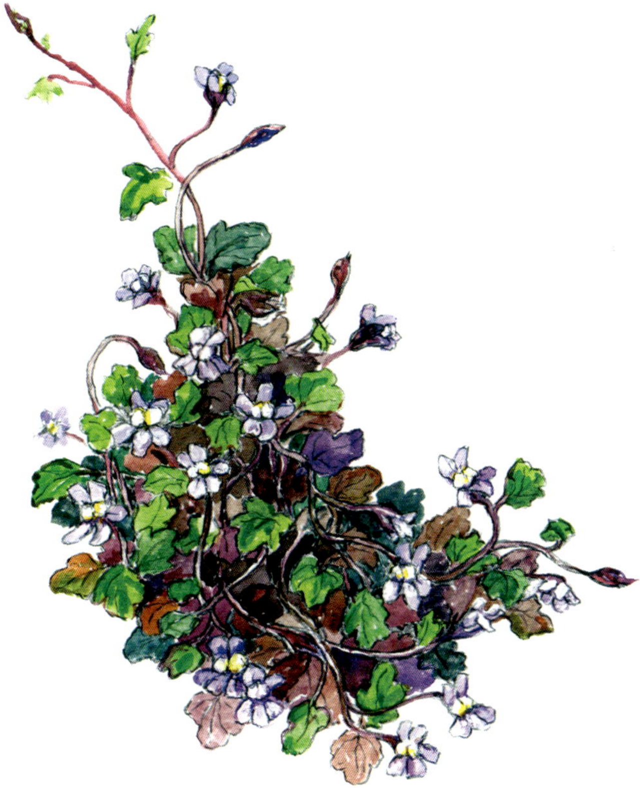

IVY-LEAVED TOADFLAX

Cymbalaria muralis *Family CYMBALARIA*

This attractive little purple flower, with yellow centre, spreads over walls and stones wherever there are buildings and shelter. As is obvious the leaves are ivy shaped. Bees love it.

Flowers May to September.

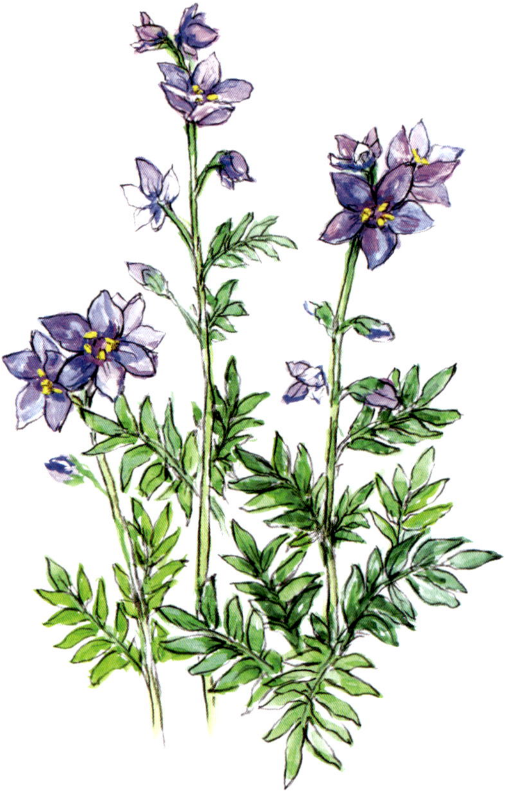

JACOB'S LADDER

Polemonium caeruleum *Family POLEMONIACEAE*

Growing one to two feet high this beautiful blue flower appears loosely at the top of the stems. It grows locally in stony places on the exposed limestone, and is a rare plant in the wild.

Flowers June to July.

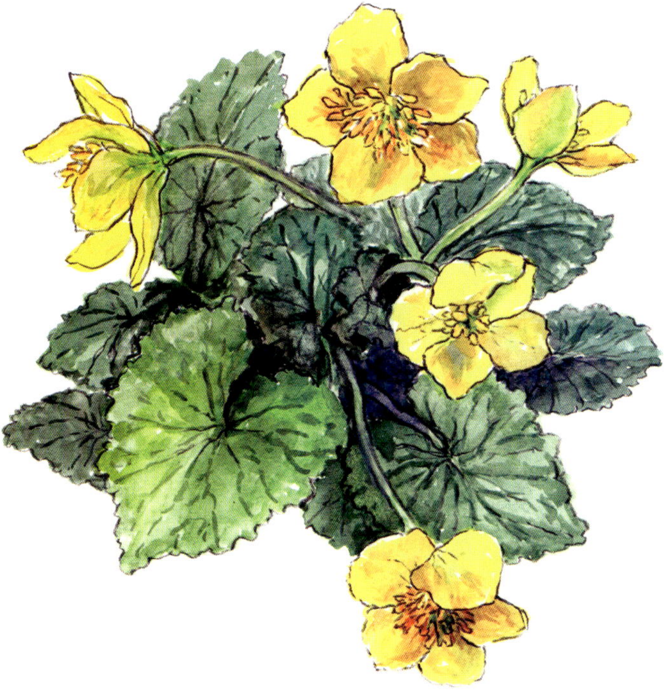

KING CUP or Marsh Marigold

Caltha palustris *Family RANUNCULACEAE*

A sturdy, large, yellow, buttercup-like flower which makes a good show along stream banks and marshy fields.

Flowers April to July.

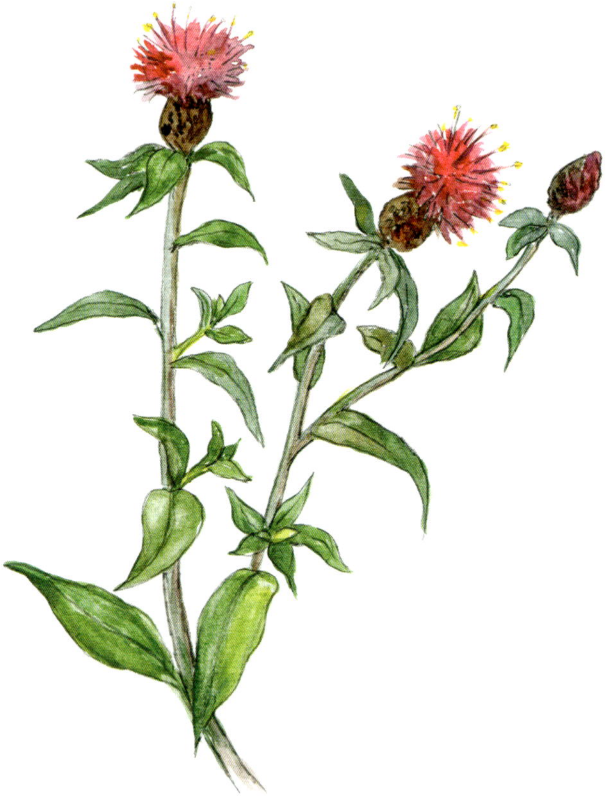

KNAPWEED or Hardhead

Centurea nigra *Family COMPOSITAE*

Very common along roadsides, and growing to as much as two feet tall, this purple, thistle-like flower (though it has no prickles) makes a cheerful appearance in long grass.

Flowers May to June.

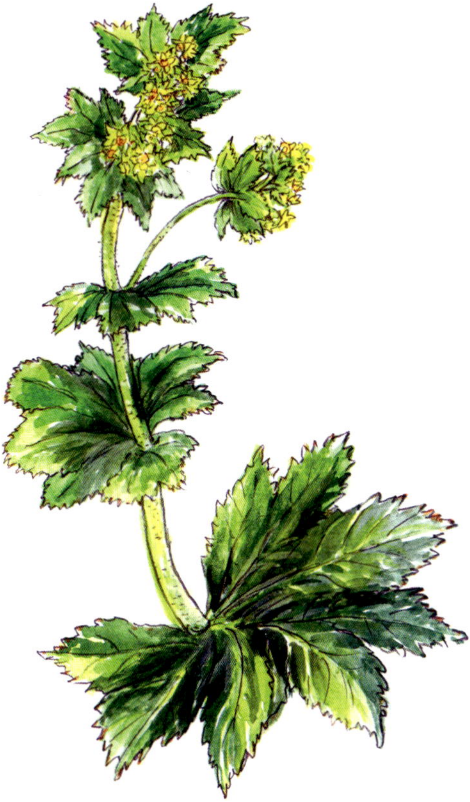

LADY'S MANTLE

Alchemilla vulgaris *Family ROSACEAE*

This plant has roundish, toothy (palmate) leaves, and tiny yellow to green flowers in unstalked clusters at the end of the stem.

Flowers from June onwards.

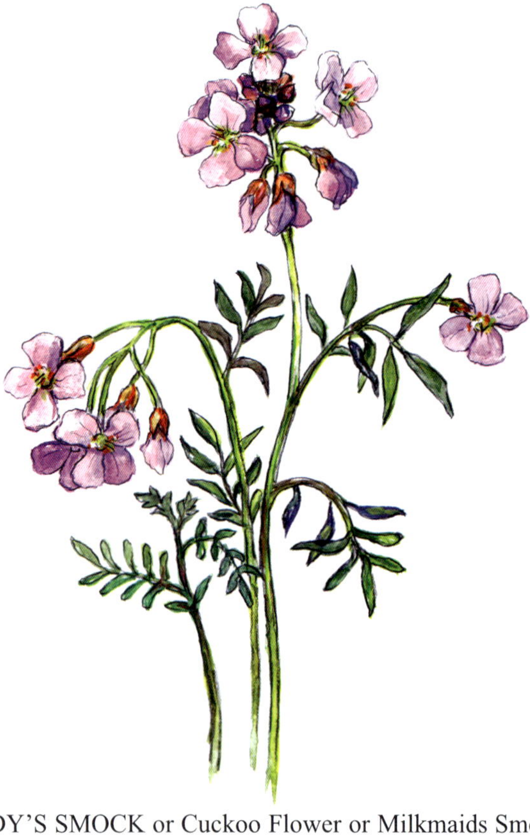

LADY'S SMOCK or Cuckoo Flower or Milkmaids Smock
Cardamine pratensis *Family CRUCIFERAE*

This perennial favours damp meadows and stream banks. It has a sweet smell from pretty pink flowers clustered at the end of smooth stems.

Flowers May to July.

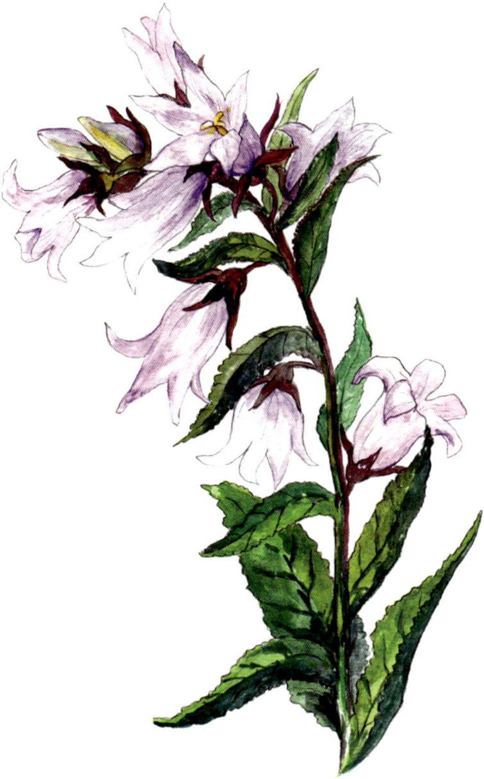

LARGE BELL FLOWER

Campanula latifolia *Family CAMPANULACEAE*

More common in the north of England than the south. Growing eighteen inches high along the valley roadsides, this flower provides a spectacular sight with blue and mauve flowers, growing in clumps among white Cow Parsley and Sweet Cecily.

Flowers July to August.

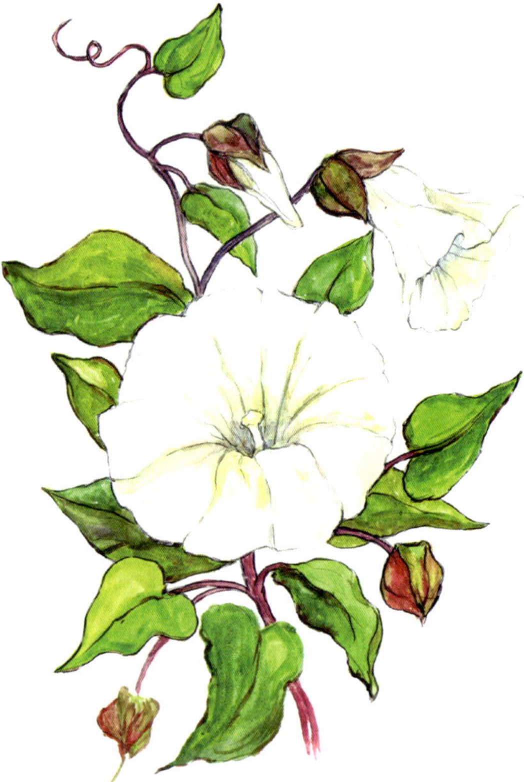

LARGE BINDWEED

Calystegia silvatica *Family CONVOLVULACEAE*

Technically an escape from gardens, it can now be found in the countryside. In the Dale it is fairly common on the roadside in the lower valley, near Richmond. It has a spectacular white flower and climbs up hedges, walls, and other plants.

Flowers July to August.

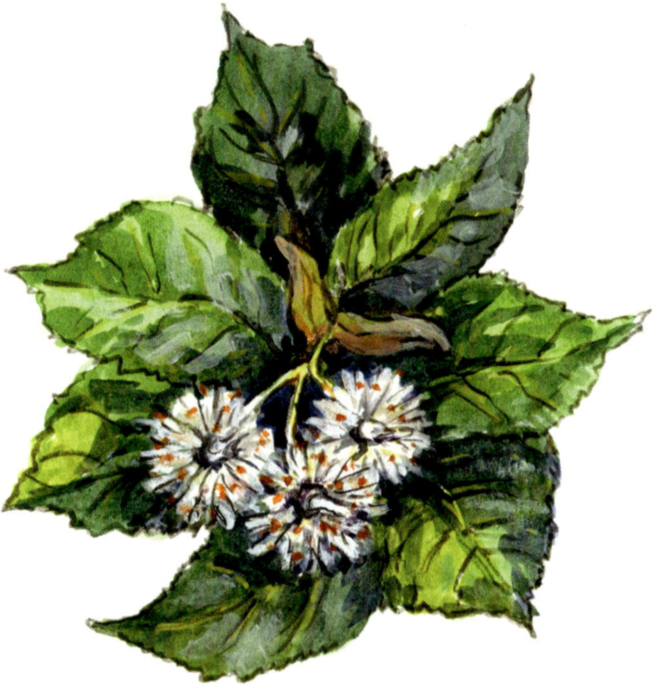

LARGE-LEAVED LIME

Tilia platyphyllos *Family TILIACEAE*

The lime trees most usually planted are hybrid. However, both species of native lime trees – small not large-leaved limes, and natural hybrids survive today on and below inaccessible cliffs in lower Swaledale.

Flowers June to July.

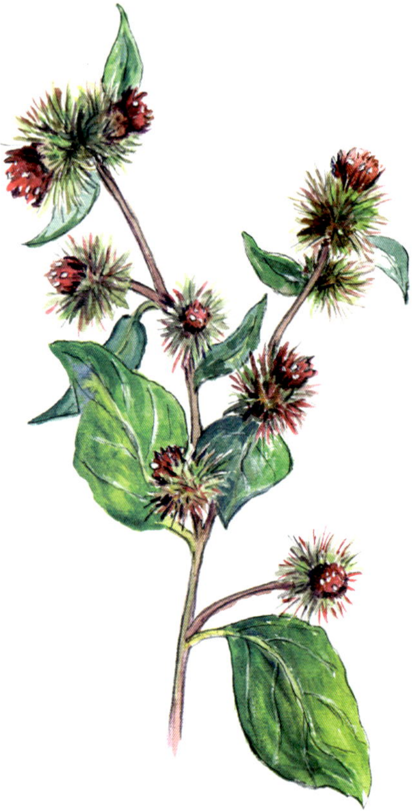

LESSER BURDOCK

Arctium minus *Family COMPOSITAE*

This bushy plant grows on wasteland and road sides. It has hollow stalks and its seed heads have little hooked spines when in fruit. At one time it was used as a herbal medicine for diseases of the skin.

Flowers July to September.

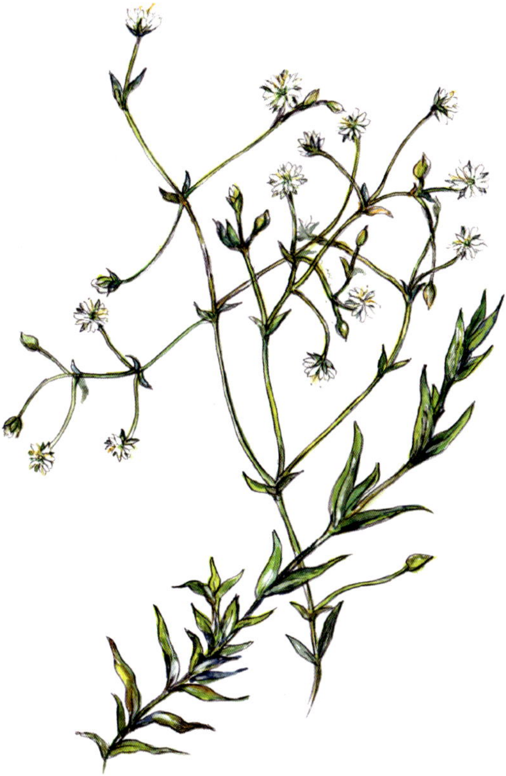

LESSER STITCHWORT or Heath Stitchwort

Stellaria graminea *Family CARYOPHYLLACEAE*

This is a common plant with small and fairly abundant white flowers. It grows in hedges and undergrowth in the valley. Stitchworts were at one time supposed to cure the 'stitch' in one's side.

Flowers May to August.

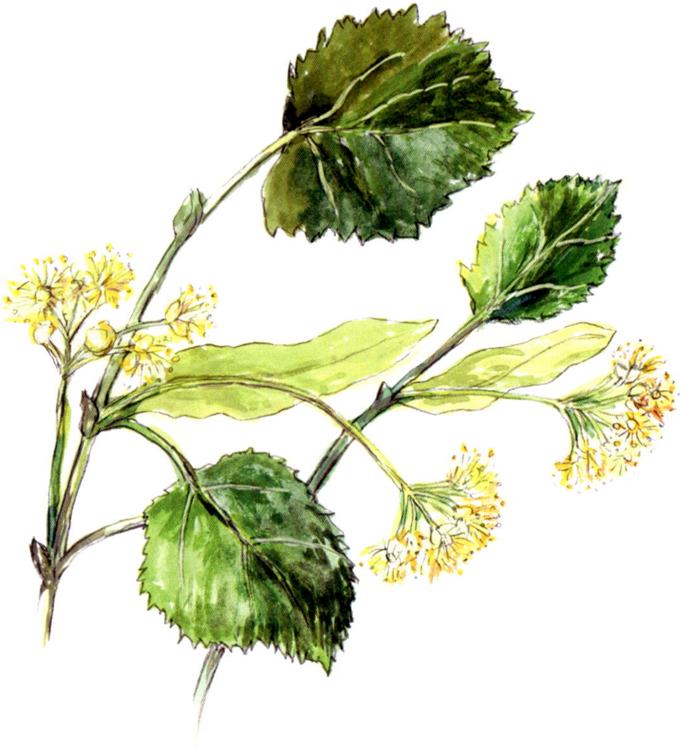

LINDEN or Lime, common

Tilia X vularis *Family TILIACEAE*

Often planted on driveways to large houses, this fine tree can be found in various places in the dales. It has bosses on the smooth trunks from which sprout many twigs, bearing the heart-shaped leaves which also cover the high branches. The delicate yellow flowers hang down and have a sweet scent. When dried these can be infused into a delicious 'tea'. The fruits are globular.

Flowers July.

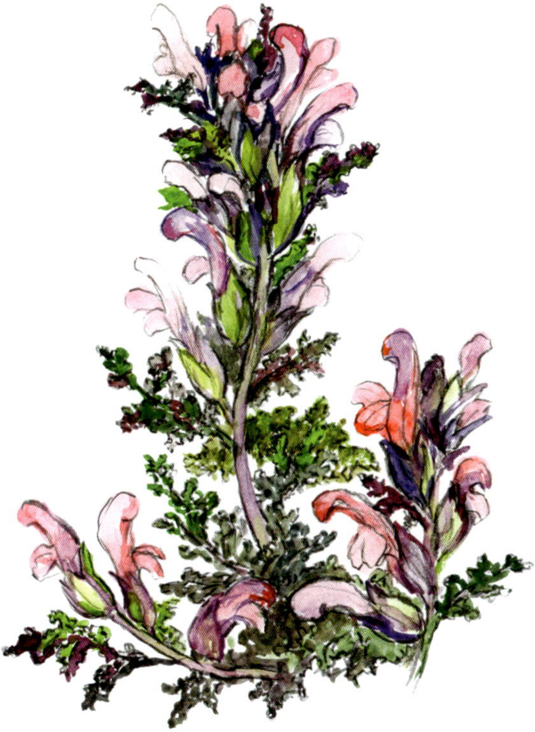

LOUSEWORT

Pedicularis sylvatica *Family SCROPHULARIACEAE*

This flower grows on the moors, damp pastures, and in mires and bogs.

Flowers April to July.

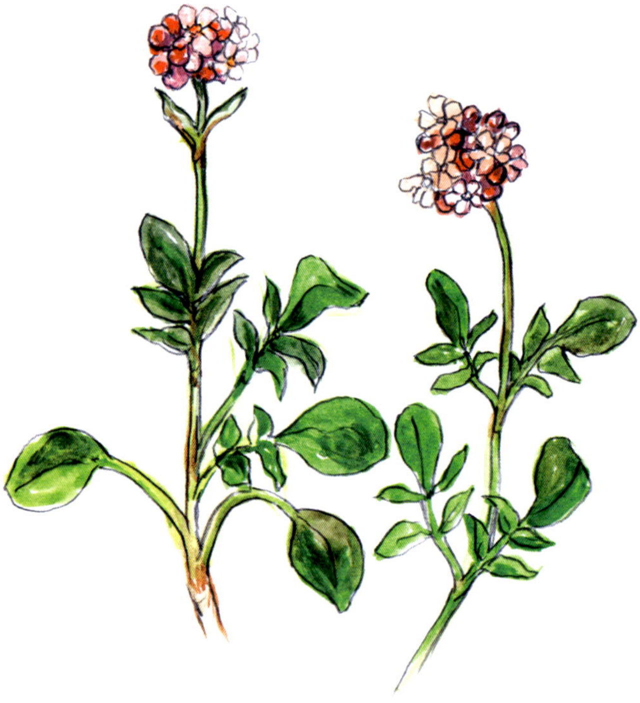

MARSH VALERIAN

Valeriana dioica *Family VALERIANACEAE*

Small pink flowers, with male and female plants separate, is most common in marshy places in the north rather than in the south.

Flowers May to June.

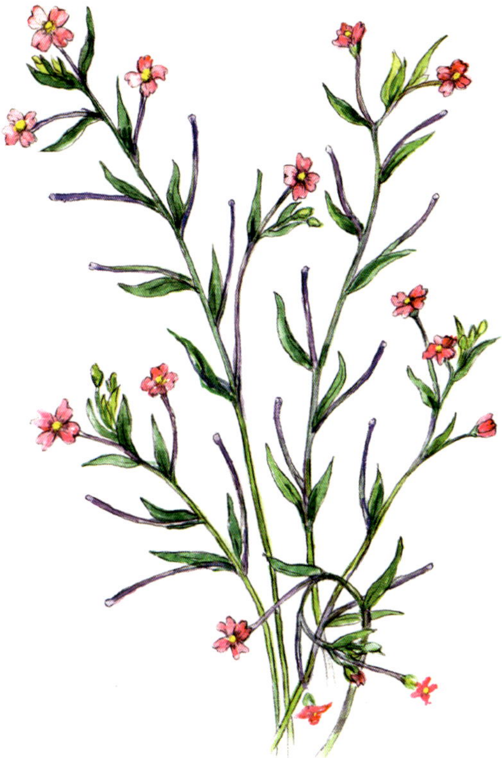

MARSH WILLOWHERB

Epilobium palustre *Family ONAGRACEAE*

A slender Willowherb about fifteen inches high, has spreading, narrow leaves with smooth edges. The flowers are small, violet/pink, and come singly at the end of the stems, drooping slightly when fully open. They have long seed heads. They like acid soils in wet places.

Flowers June to August.

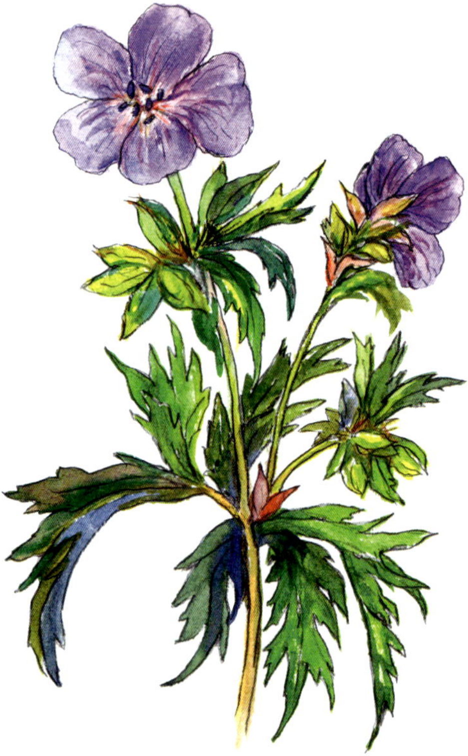

MEADOW CRANESBILL

Geranium pratense *Family GERANIACEAE*

This handsome plant has largish bright blue to violet flowers, and reddish stalks. The leaves are deeply lobed, and the fruit stalks bent downwards when ripe. It grows in grassy places, particularly in the hay meadows.

Flowers June to August.

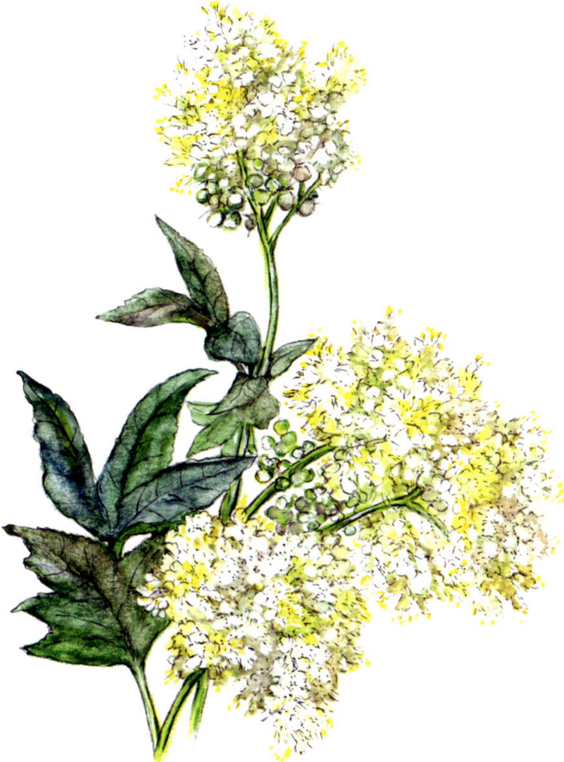

MEADOWSWEET

Flipendula ulmaria *Family ROSACEAE*

A sweet smelling, common plant, with heads of cream coloured, clustered little flowers on strong tall stems, among silvery/green pinnate leaves. It grows lushly on stream banks and boggy places, reaching nearly three feet high.

Flowers June to September.

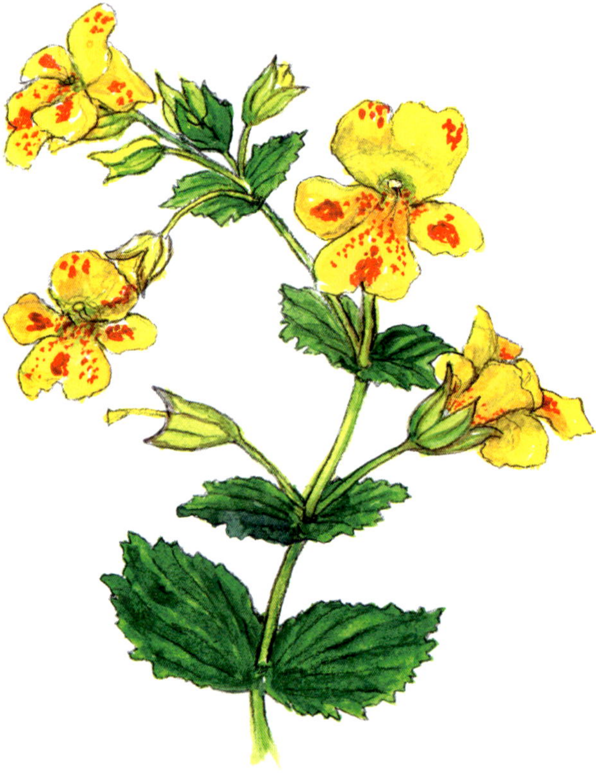

MONKEY FLOWER

Mimulus guttatus *Family SCROPHULARIACEAE*

With a yellow or yellow with dark red markings, this attractive flower thrives in shallow stream beds or on damp moss and moist ground. It is found in the dale.

Flowers June to September.

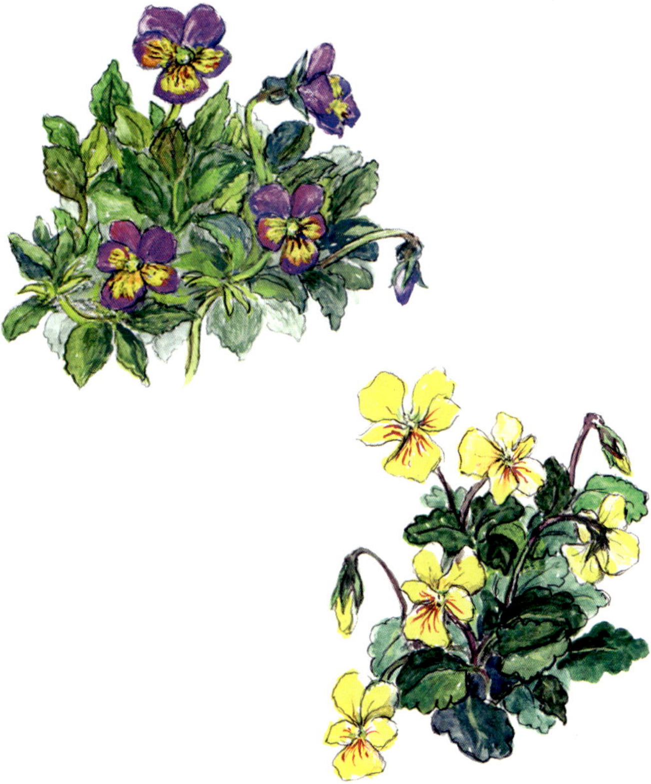

MOUNTAIN PANSY or Heartsease

Viola lutea *Family VIOLACEAE*

This pretty little flower, like a miniature garden pansy, covers patches of short grass on the hillsides with yellow and purple flowers. It is particularly common in northern hills of England.

Flowers May to August.

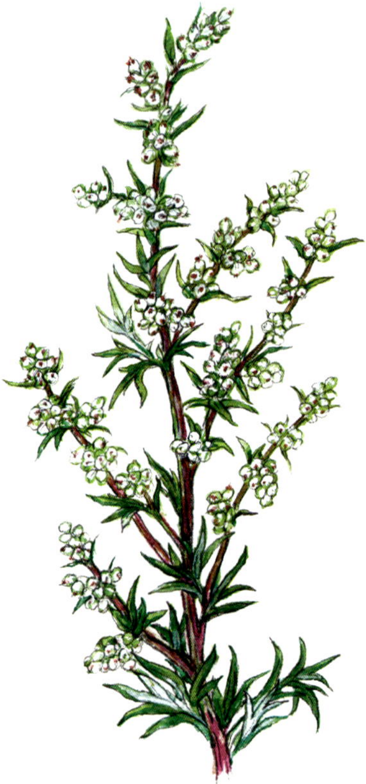

MUGWORT

Artemisia vulgaris *Family COMPOSITAE*

This tall plant spreads along roadsides, branching freely with flower stems reaching three or four feet high. The flowers are small, egg-shaped and whitish/green. The dark green leaves have a downy white underside. The plant has quite an aromatic smell.

Flowers August to September.

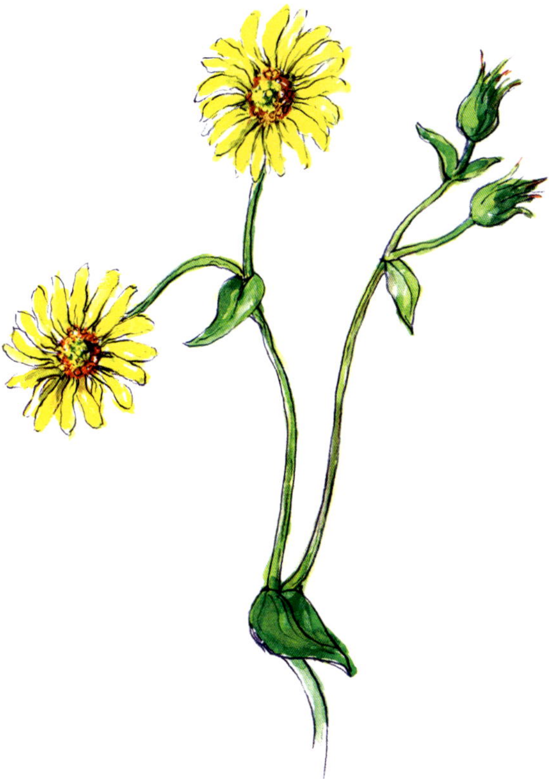

NIPPLEWORT

Lapsana communis *Family COMPOSITAE*

This plant is an annual which grows to two foot high. It has stiff leafy stems with pointed oval and toothed leaves. Branched flower heads come on long thin stalks and are yellow, like tiny dandelions. It grows in shady places in the dales.

Flowers July to September.

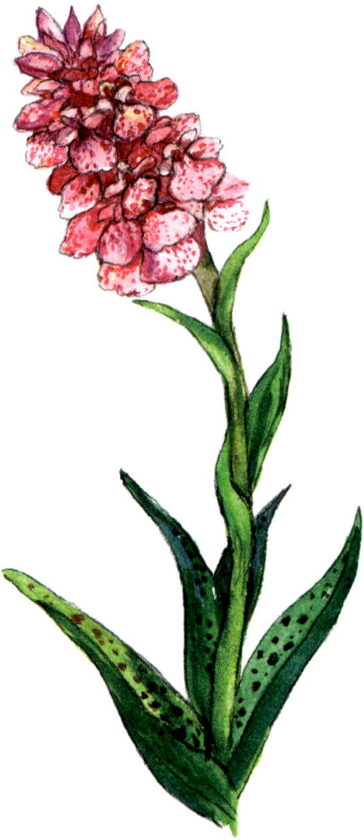

NORTHERN MARSH ORCHID

Dactylorhiza purpurella *Family ORCHIDACEAE*

These plants prefer wet places, so are usually found near the river and in marshes. They hybrid easily so often are difficult to identify in that their colour can vary from fleshy pink to purple. They sometimes have spotted leaves.

Flowers May to July.

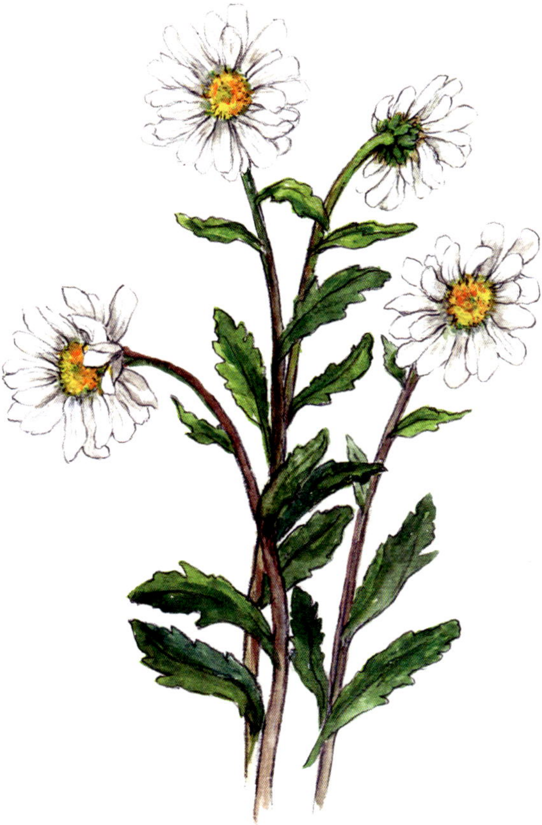

OX-DAISY or Marguerite

Leucanthemum vulgare *COMPOSITAE Family ASTERACEAE*

This large and tall white daisy flower is found in roadside verges and fields in the dale.

Flowers July to August.

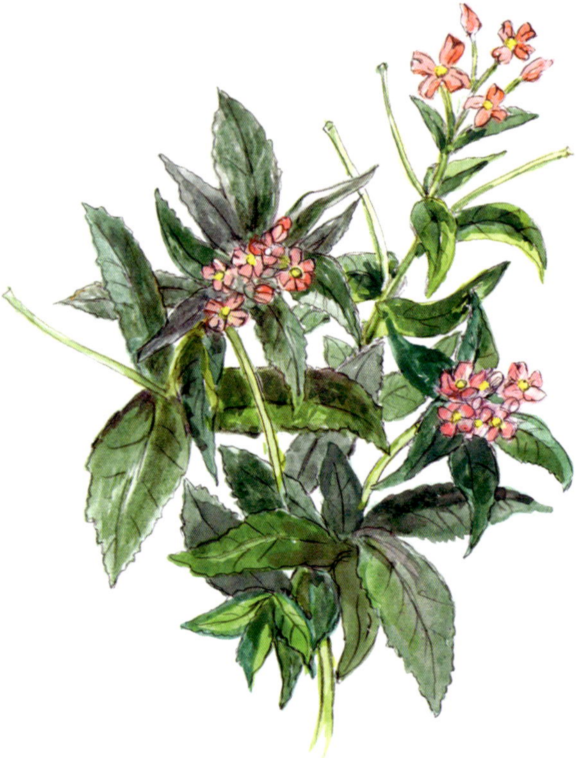

PALE WILLOWHERB

Epilobium roseum *Family ONAGRACEAE*

This southern species is found as a garden weed in the Yorkshire Dales.

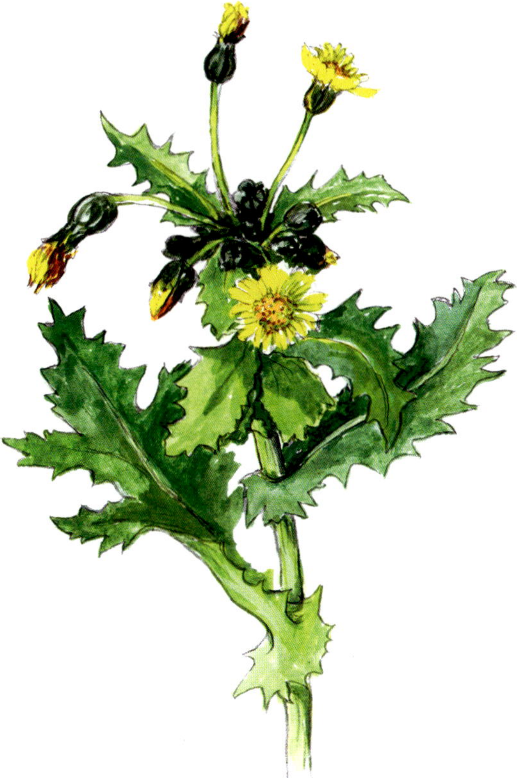

PRICKLY SOW THISTLE

Sonchus asper *Family COMPOSITAE*

This yellow dandelion-like flower appears from a long green bud on slender stems at the top of the main stalk. The leaves, which are spiky cling closely up the stalk. It grows on wasteland and verges, liking disturbed ground.

Flowers June to August.

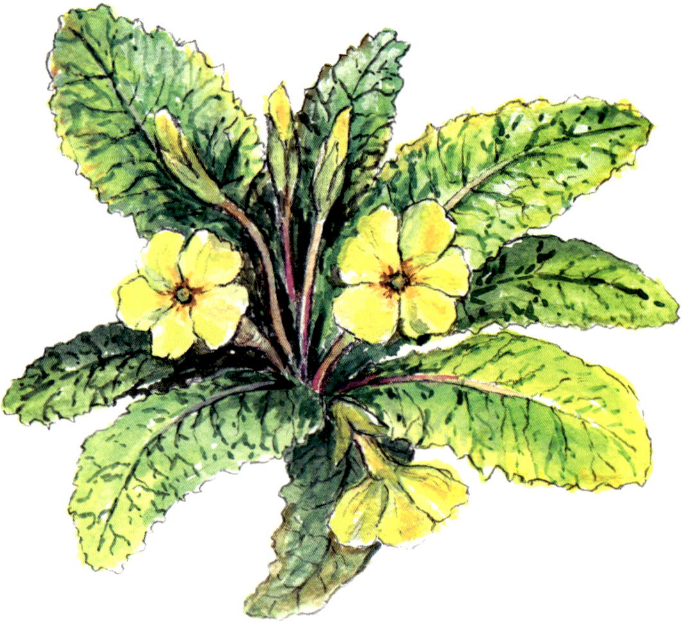

PRIMROSE

Primula vulgaris *Family PRIMULACEAE*

This early spring flower with its sweet scent, grows on banks and woodlands along the dale and lower hills. The pale yellow flower appears singly on separate stems rising from the somewhat crinkly leaves which lie on the ground.

Flowers March to May.

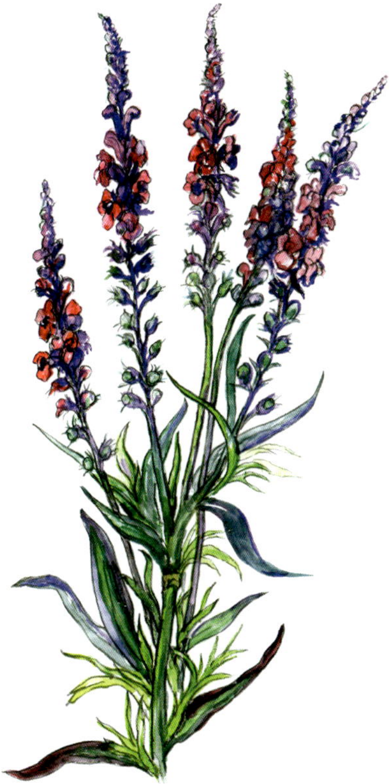

PURPLE TOADFLAX

Linaria purpurea *Family SCROPHULARIACEAE*

Dense little violet flowers form a straight spike which can reach eighteen inches high. It has narrow leaves towards its base. It is often found as a garden weed and grows where soil has been disturbed. It is rare in the dale.

Flowers June to September.

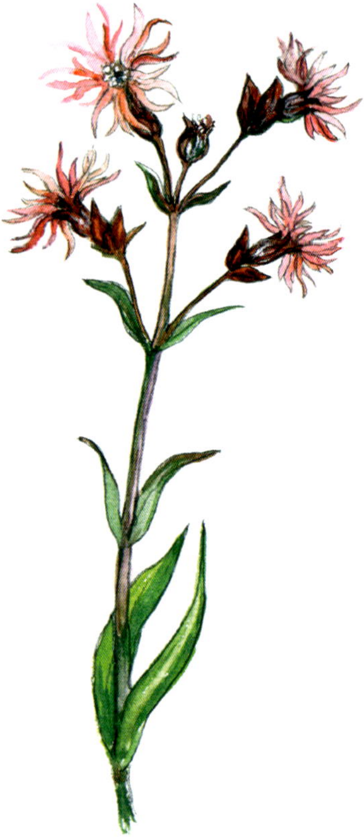

RAGGED ROBIN

Lychnis flos-cuculi *Family CARYOPHYLLACEAE*

As the name implies this plant has rather untidy pink flowers with deeply divided petals. It grows fairly commonly in damp meadows and hedgerows. It attracts bees and butterflies.

Flowers May to July.

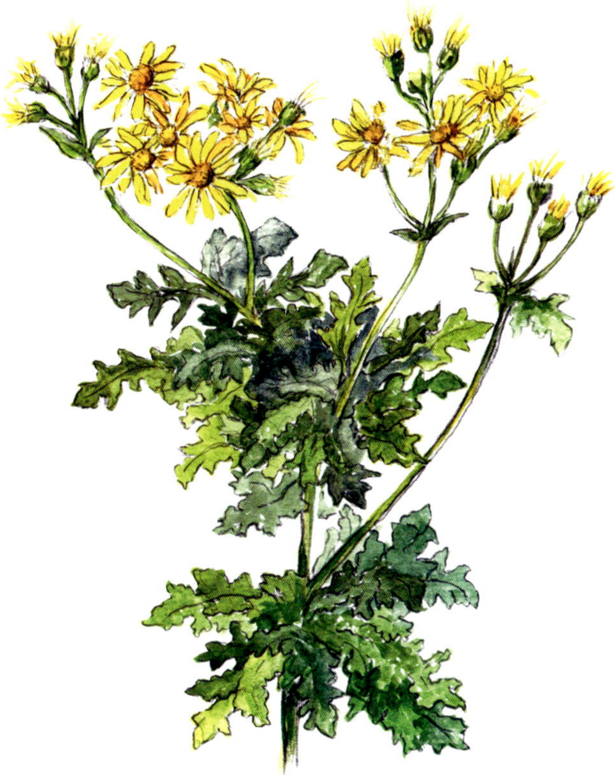

RAGWORT

Senecio jacobaea *Family COMPOSITAE*

A bright yellow daisy-like flower at the top of stems eighteen inches to two feet tall, it grows in pastures and roadsides. It must be removed by farmers as it is poisonous to some animals.

Flowers June to October.

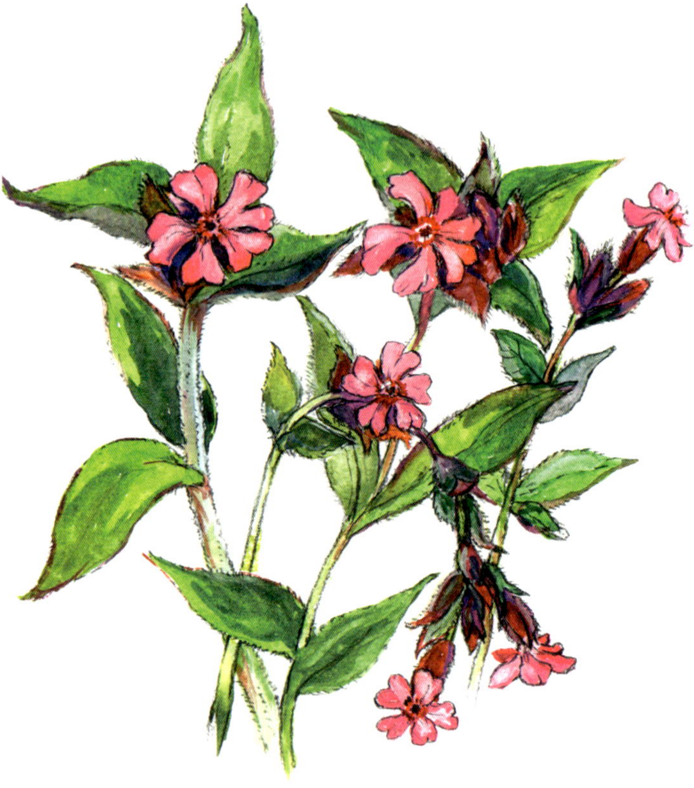

RED CAMPION

Silene dioica *Family CARYOPHYLLACEAE*

This bright red/pink flower grows in clumps in woods and hedges, and can also be found higher on the hillsides among rocky slopes. Male and female flowers grow separately on different plants.

Flowers April to August.

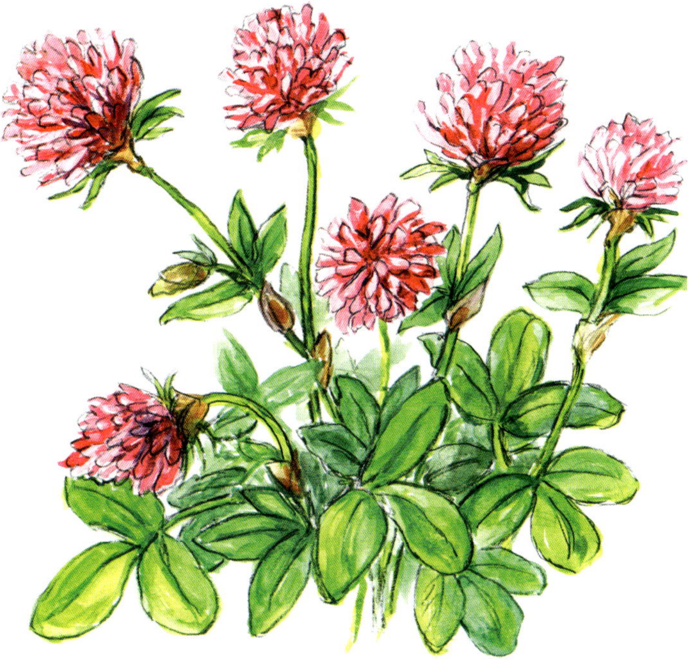

RED CLOVER

Trifolium pratense *Family LEGUMINOSAE*

This familiar red clover with its round cluster of sweet smelling flowers is familiar all over the country. It thrives in the dales in hay meadows and roadsides. It has numbers of three oval leaves together, which sometimes are marked with a white crescent.

Flowers May to October.

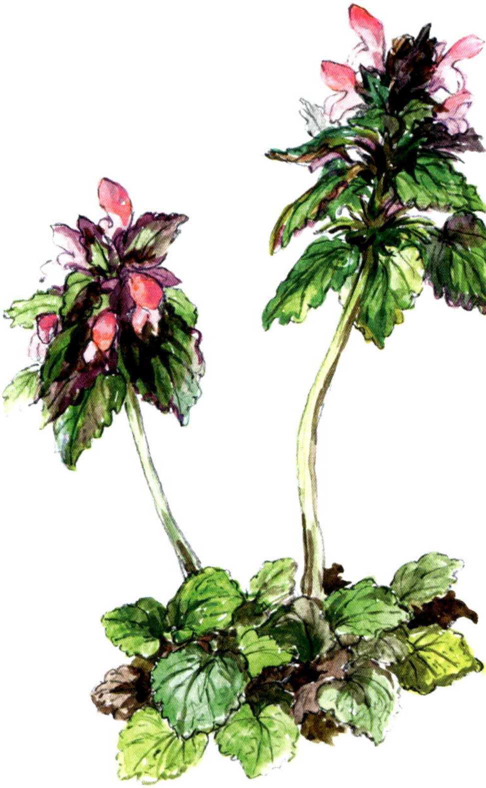

RED DEAD-NETTLE

Lamium purpureum *Family LABIATAE*

This downy dead-nettle does not sting. It has a purple/pink flower which alternates with the leaves up the square stem. It grows to two feet high on disturbed ground in the valley, and in fields.

In flower throughout most of the year.

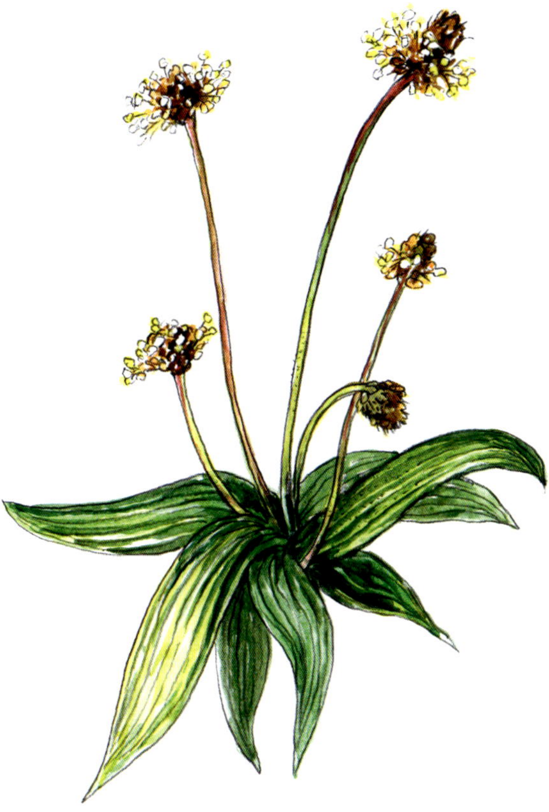

RIBWORT PLANTAIN

Plantago lanceolata *Family PLANTAGINACEAE*

A very familiar plant in grass and meadows. It flowers in stubby spikes, blackish brown, or greenish before flowering, and pale brown afterwards with pale yellow or purple anthers.

Flowers from April onwards.

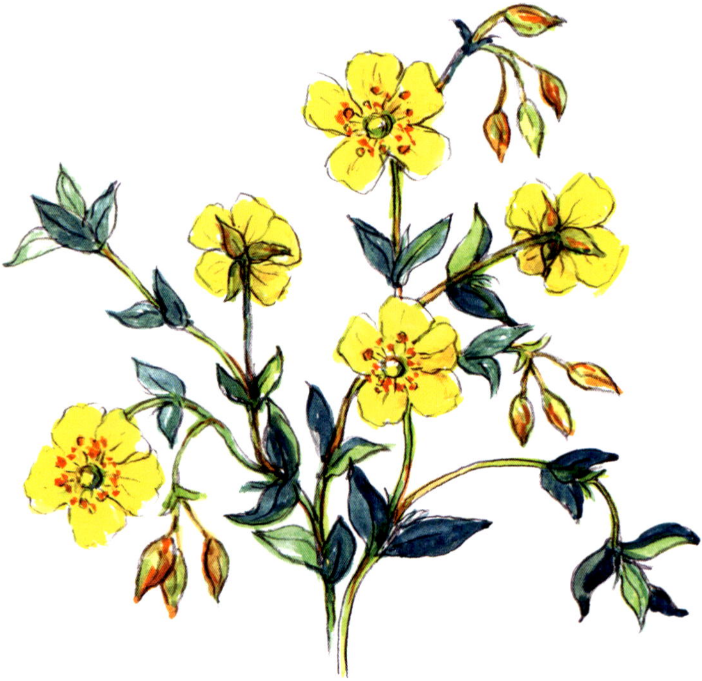

ROCK ROSE (Common)

Helianthemum nummularium *Family CISTACEAE*

This small yellow flower flourishes on limestone spreading in dense clumps. It is however not a rose. Its Latin name means ‘sun flower’ because it only fully opens in sunshine. The small dark evergreen leaves have white hairs underneath.

Flowers May onwards.

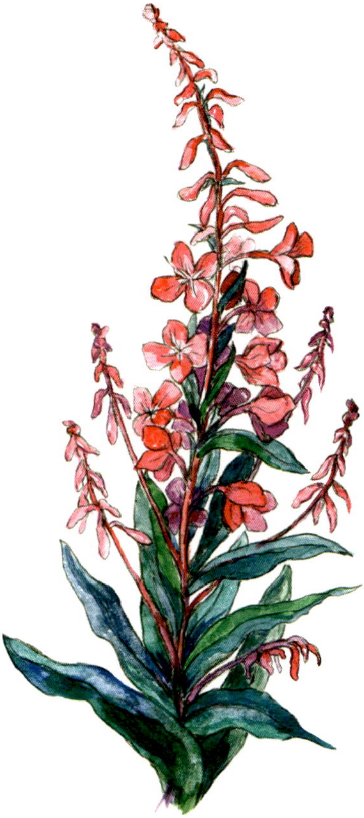

ROSEBAY WILLOWHERB

Epilobium augustifolium *Family ONAGRACEAE*

This tall plant is a feature in late summer and autumn. Known sometimes as 'fireweed' its blazing pink covers areas where trees have been felled and other waste ground on the slopes of the dale.

Flowers from July to September.

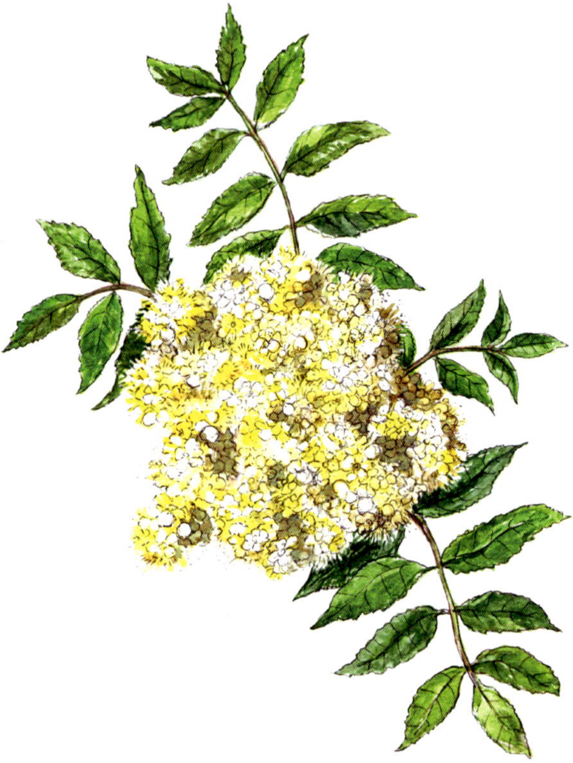

ROWAN or Mountain Ash

Sorbus aucuparia *Family ROSACEAE*

As this small tree's name indicates, it can be found at all elevations throughout the two dales. The flat flower heads are made up of clusters of small white flowers, but it is the scarlet red berries which make it so distinctive especially when the fringed leaved are turning orange and yellow in autumn.

Flowers from May to June.

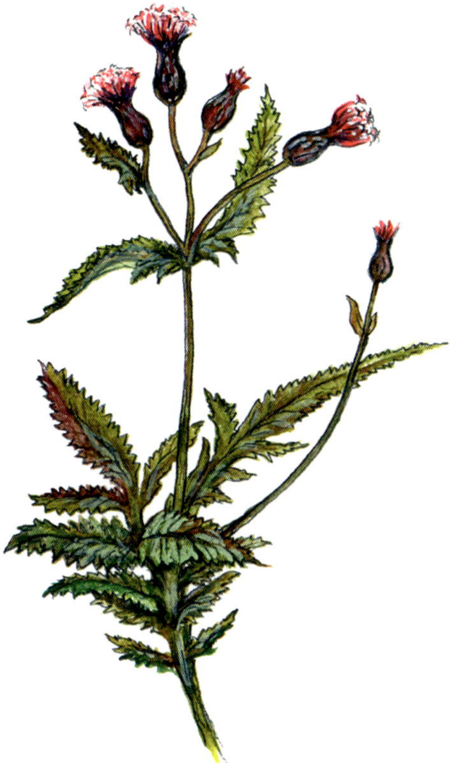

SAW-WORT

Serratula tinctoria *Family COMPOSITAE*

Thistle-like purple flowers come loosely at the top of this one to two foot tall plant. The stalks are stiff and the finely toothed leaves are lobed , but almost undivided, It grows in long grass, open woodland and heathy places. It is rare in the dale.

Flowers from July to September.

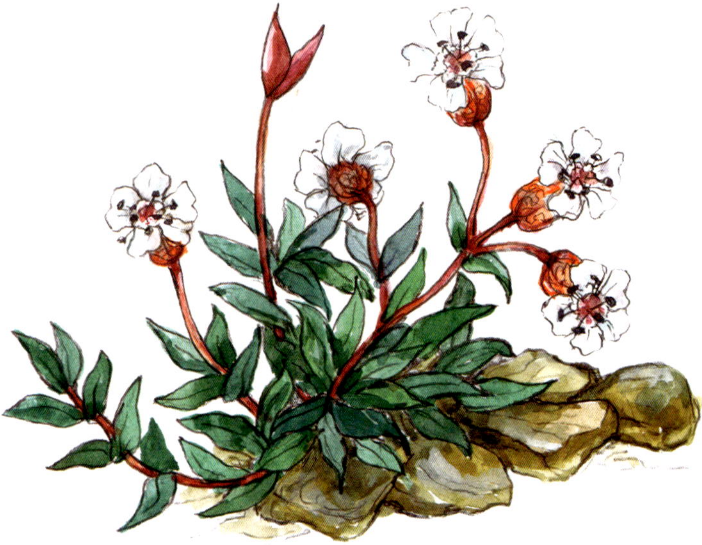

SEA CAMPION

Silene maritima *Family CARYOPHYLLACEAE*

In spite of the name of this pretty white flower with its broad petals, it can sometimes be found on high ground in stony places on hill tops and mountains, away from the sea. It is very rare in Swaledale.

Flowers from June to August.

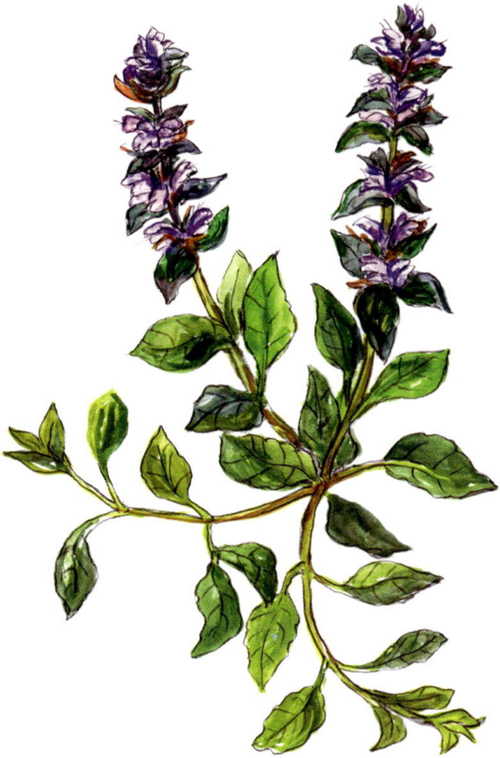

SELF-HEAL

Prunella vulgaris *Family LABIATAE*

The creeping stem roots and upright flowering stems, grow in grassland and woods. The violet to pink flowers appear at the top of the stem. It was once thought to promote healing without the need for a doctor.

Flowers from June to August.

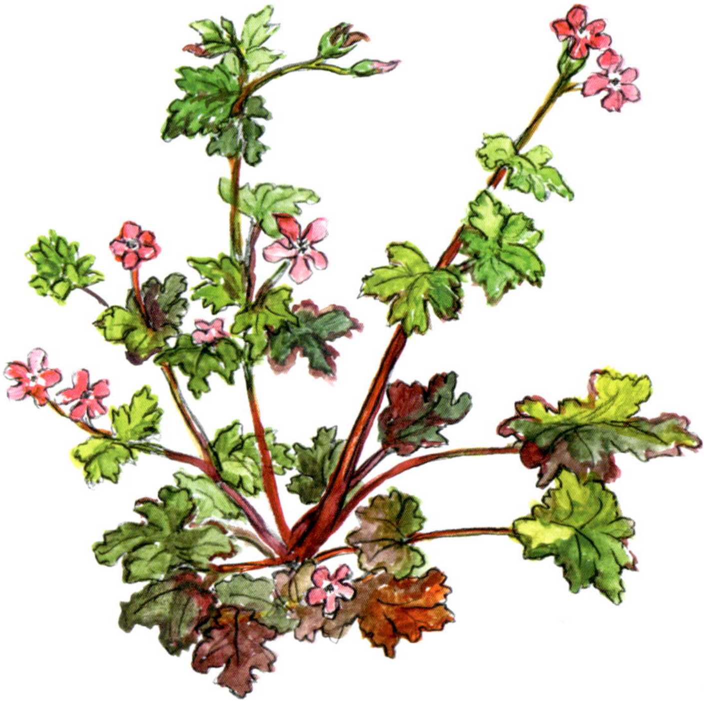

SHINING CRANESBILL

Geranium lucidum *Family GERANIACEAE*

This small pink flower has shiny leaves and stems, and the usual distinctive 'crane's beak' common to all cranesbill flowers when in seed. It grows in dry, stony places and walls.

Flowers from April to August.

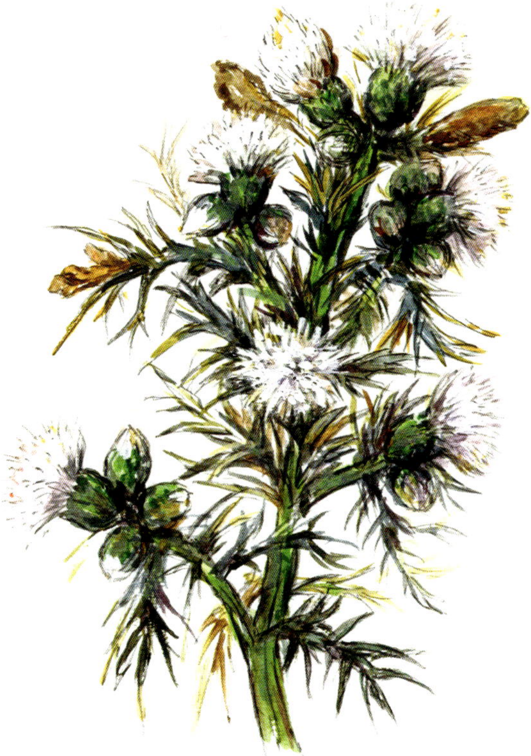

SLENDER THISTLE

Carduus tenuiflorus *Family COMPOSITAE*

This is a very spiny thistle, with long prickles up its stem and on its leaves. The flower heads are spiky and narrow and bear purple to mauve flowers. It grows in hedges and on grassland on the dale-sides.

Flowers from June to August.

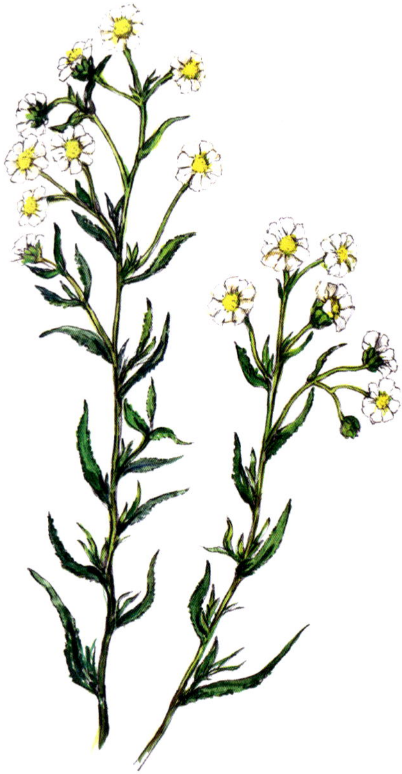

SNEEZEWORT

Achillea ptarmica *Family COMPOSITAE*

Related to Yarrow this white flower with a yellow centre, has a looser flower head. It has toothy leaves which cling to the main stem where flower stems rise. It enjoys heavy acid soil in low places.

Flowers from July to September.

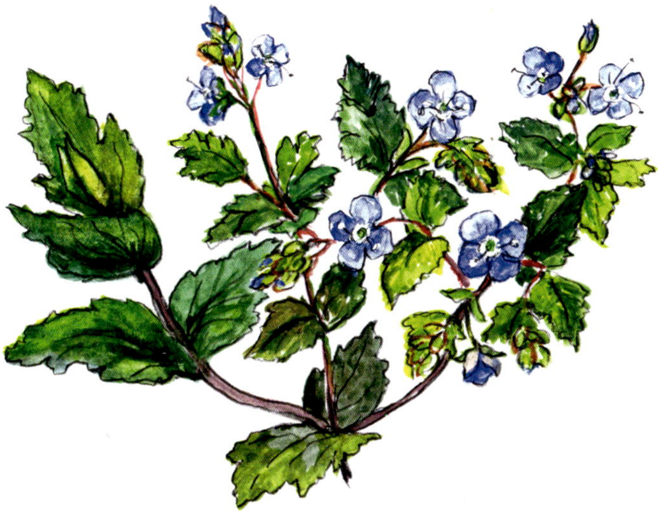

SPEEDWELL GERMANDER or Bird's eye speedwell

Veronica chamaedrys *Family SCROPHULARIACEAE*

This common bright blue flower with white centre, grows in grassy places and woods throughout the valley.

Flowers from April to July.

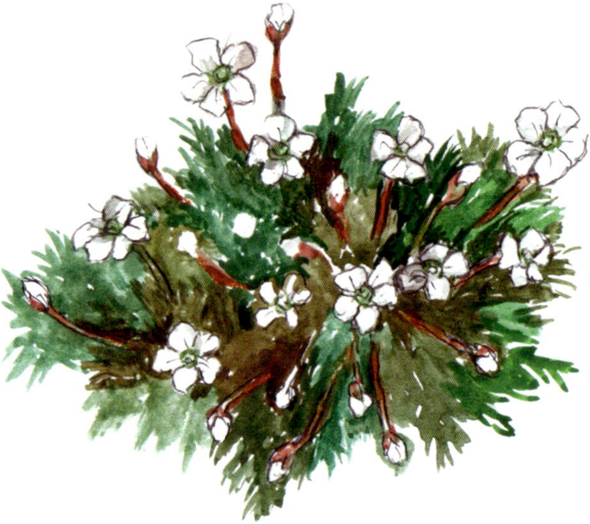

SPRING SANDWORT

Minuartia verna *Family CARYOPHYLLACAE*

Small narrow leaved and white flowered cushions of this heavy metal tolerant plant are found on the spoilheaps of the lead mines.

Flowers from April to July.

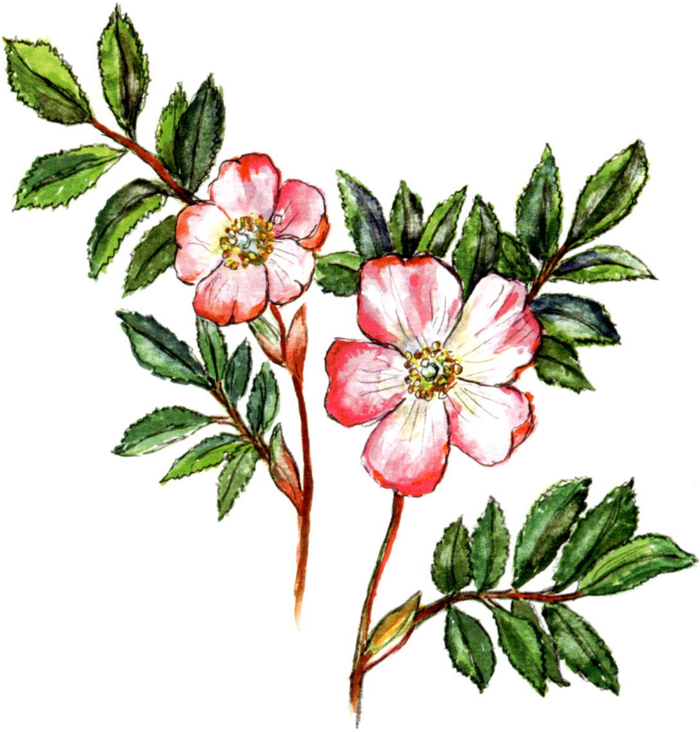

SWEET BRIAR

Rosa rubiginosa *Family ROSACEAE*

This shrub favours hedgerows and woods. It has a bright pink flower (occasionally white) and hooked prickles on its stems and flower stalks. When crushed the leaves have an aromatic smell. The hips are rounded and an orange/red. It is very rare in Swaledale.

Flowers from June to July.

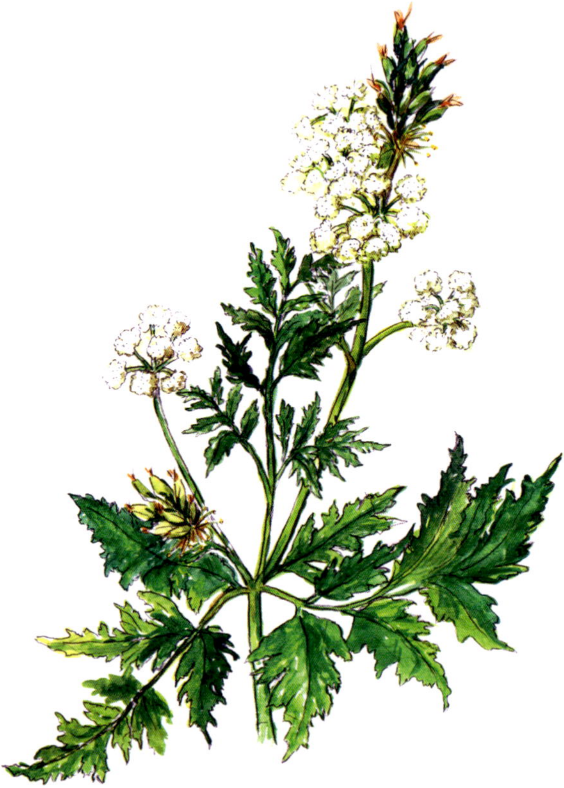

SWEET CECILY

Myrrhis odorata *Family UMBELLIFERAE*

This frothy white flower grows abundantly on Swaledale roadsides. It is very rare in the south of the country. When crushed it has a strong aniseed scent.

Flowers from May to June.

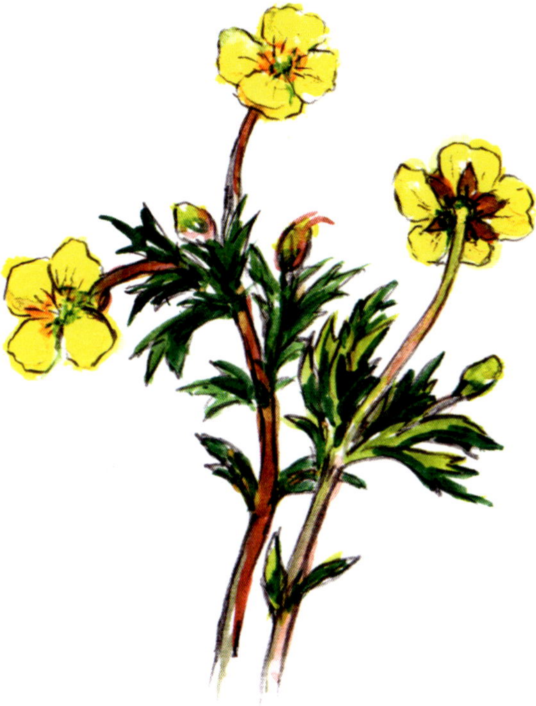

TORMENTIL

Potentilla erecta *Family ROSACEAE*

A slender, downy perennial with long stems and small yellow flowers; it likes acid soil on heaths and moors and grassy places on the hillsides. It was believed to be a cure for diarrhoea and sore throats.

Flowers from June to September.

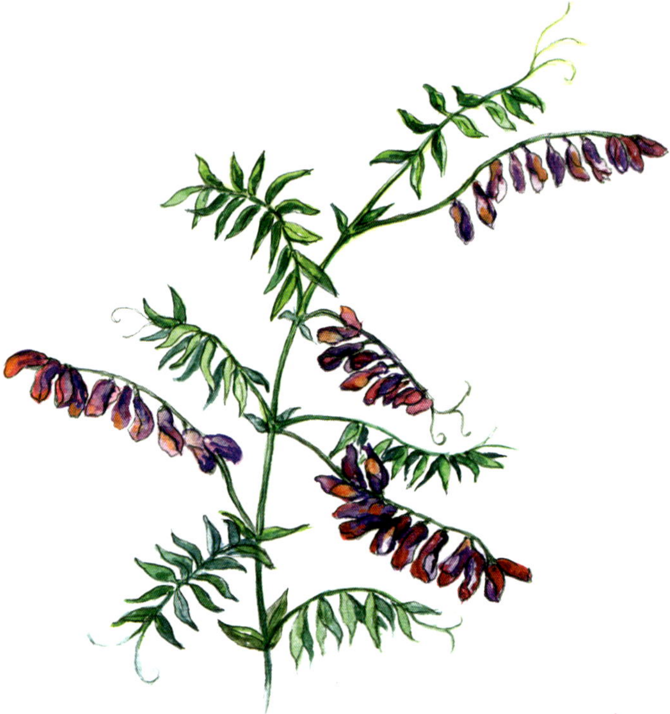

TUFTED VETCH

Vicia cracca *Family LEGUMINOSAE*

With its tendrils it is found climbing over hedges and bushes and long grass in the valley. Its flowers, which are purple, hang from one side of its stems.

Flowers from June to August.

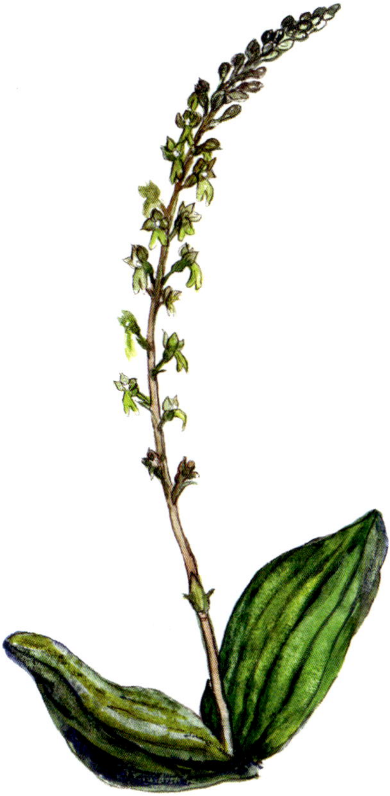

TWAYBLADE

Listera ovata *Family ORCHIDACEAE*

This secretive flower is hard to find, with its small green flowers, however it can be easily identified by its two distinctive, large oval-shaped leaves, and can be found on roadsides, verges and pastures.

Flowers from June to July.

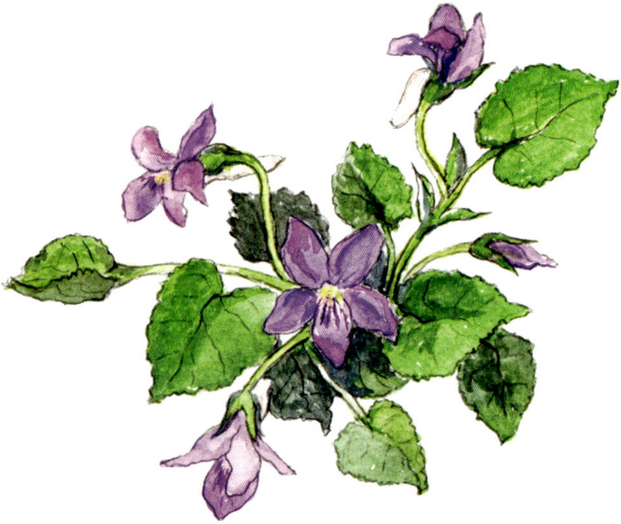

VIOLET or Common Dog Violet

Viola riviniana *Family VIOLACEAE*

The commonest violet to be found. It has blue/violet flowers and heart-shaped leaves. It grows in short grass, woods and hedges.

Flowers from April to June.

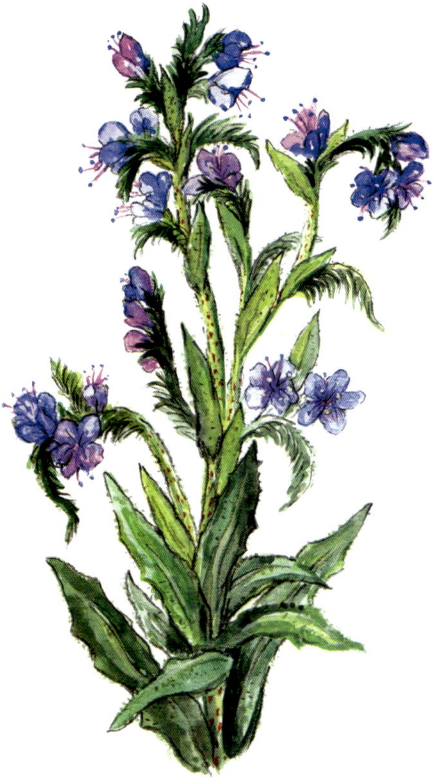

VIPER'S BUGLOSS

Echium vulgare *Family BORAGINACEAE*

This roughly hairy biennial grows to one or two feet high. The flowers droop in pink clusters before opening to a vivid blue with purple and pink centres. It favours dry light soil, and can be found anywhere except on the higher hills.

Flowers from June to September.

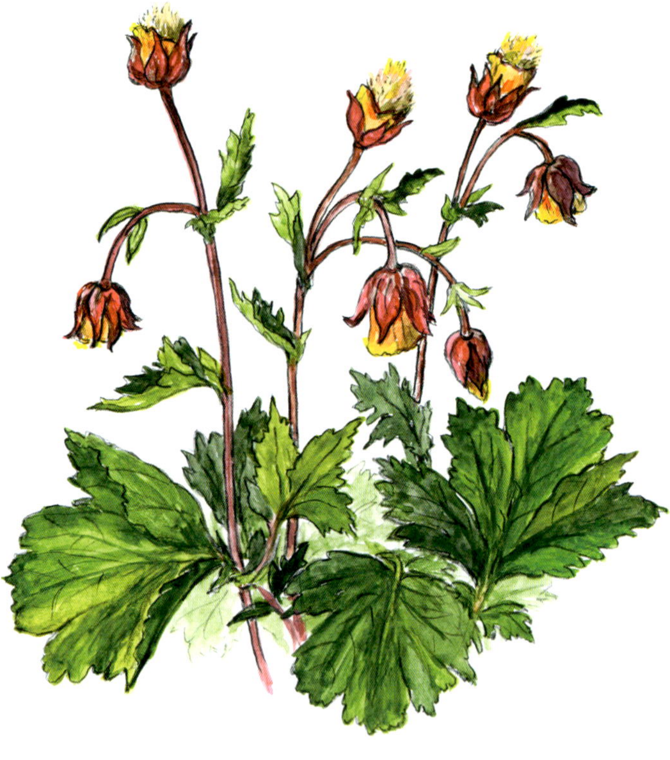

WATER AVENS

Geum rivale *Family ROSACEAE*

This pretty downy perennial grows fairly commonly in damp ditches and stream beds in the valley. The flowers, which are reddish, hang from the end of its stems.

Flowers from June to August.

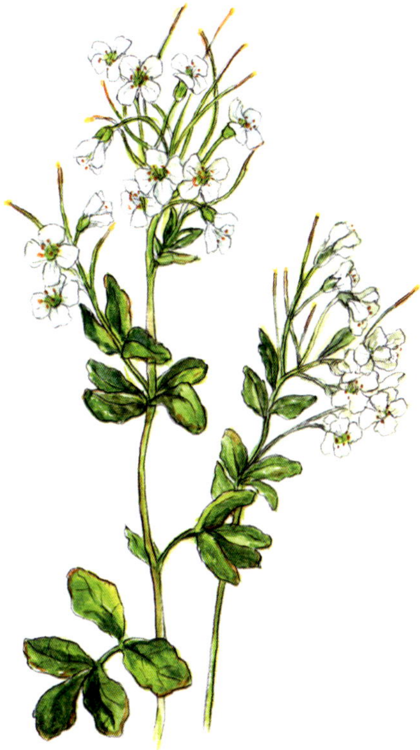

WATERCRESS

Nasturtium officinale *Family CRUCIFERAE*

The swift flowing Swale and Arkle are not the most hospitable places for these plants, but they may be found in lazier streams or ponds where the cress can take root. The plant has white flowers whose petals are narrower at their base. The pinnate, green leaves remain all year.

Flowers from June onwards.

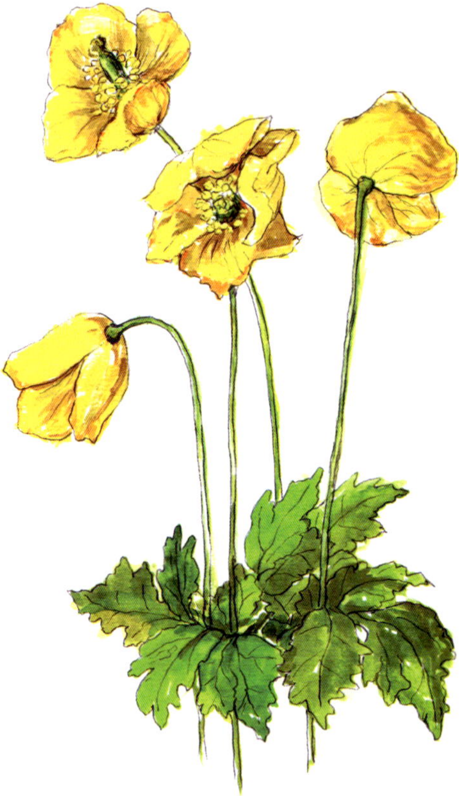

WELSH POPPY

Meconopsis cambrica *Family PAPAVERACEAE*

Found in damp, shady places. It has a delicate yellow flower which tends to nod, rather than open fully.

Flowers from June to August.

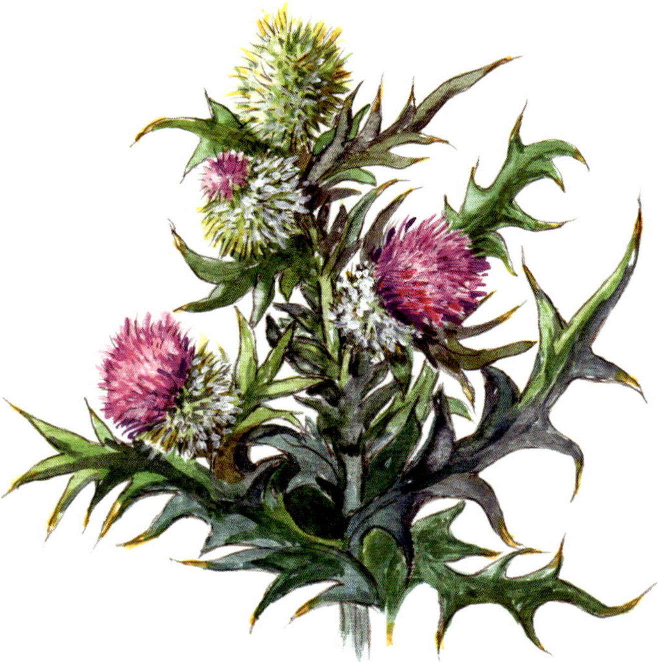

WELTED THISTLE

Carduus acanthoides *Family COMPOSITAE*

This thistle is rarer in the north than the south, it can be found on the lower hillsides, and in hedges. It has clusters of mauve flowers, sometimes white, at the top of extremely prickly stems and leaves.

Flowers from May to September.

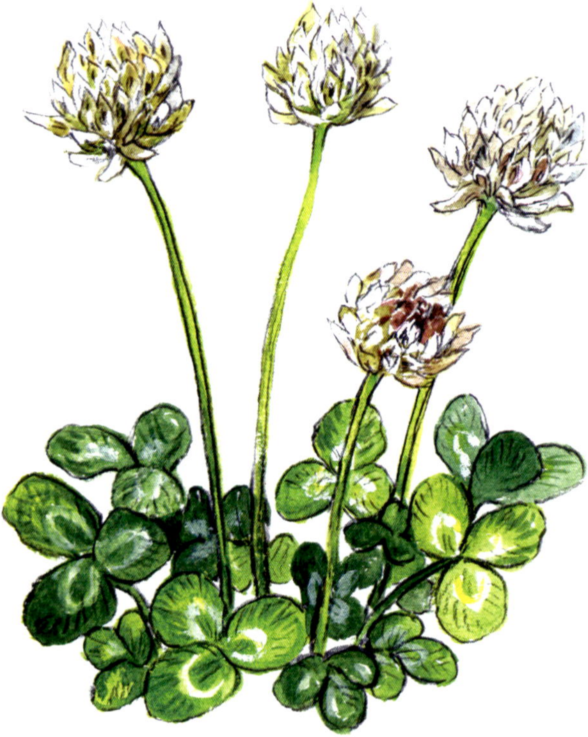

WHITE CLOVER or Dutch clover

Trifolium repens *Family LEGUMINOSAE*

A variation on the more common mauve clover. Quite common in grassy places and garden lawns.

Flowers from May to September.

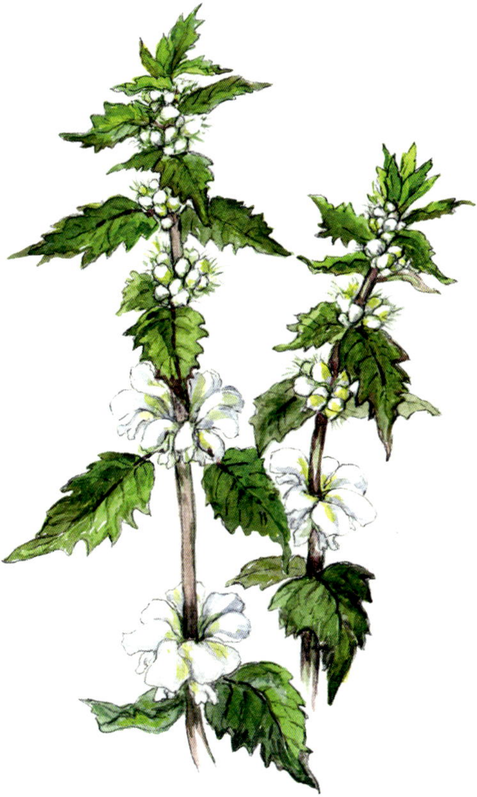

WHITE DEAD-NETTLE

Lamium album *Family LABIATAE*

Although not so common in the north, this hairy stemmed white flower can be found on road sides and ditches. It does not sting.

Flowers from May to November.

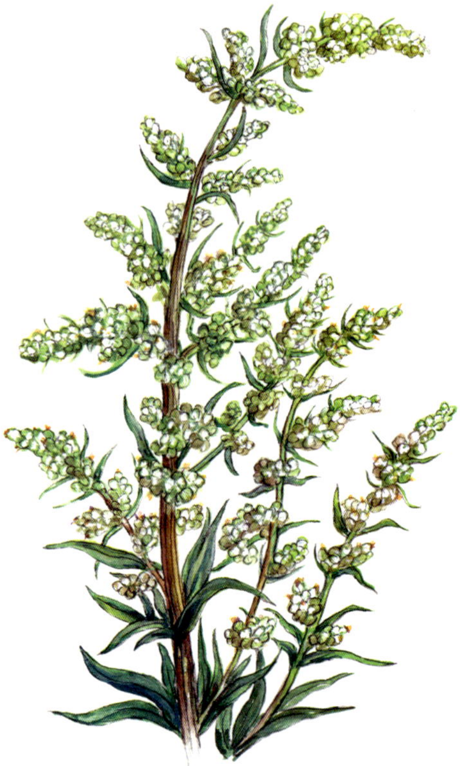

WHITE GOOSEFOOT or Fat-hen.
Chenopodium album *Family CHENOPODIACEAE*

A tall plant on roadsides and waste land, this well branched plant bears whitish, mealy shoots and narrow sword-like leaves, though towards the base the leaves are diamond shaped and toothed. The insignificant pallid flowers cluster on spikes from small leaves on the main stems.

Flowers from June to September.

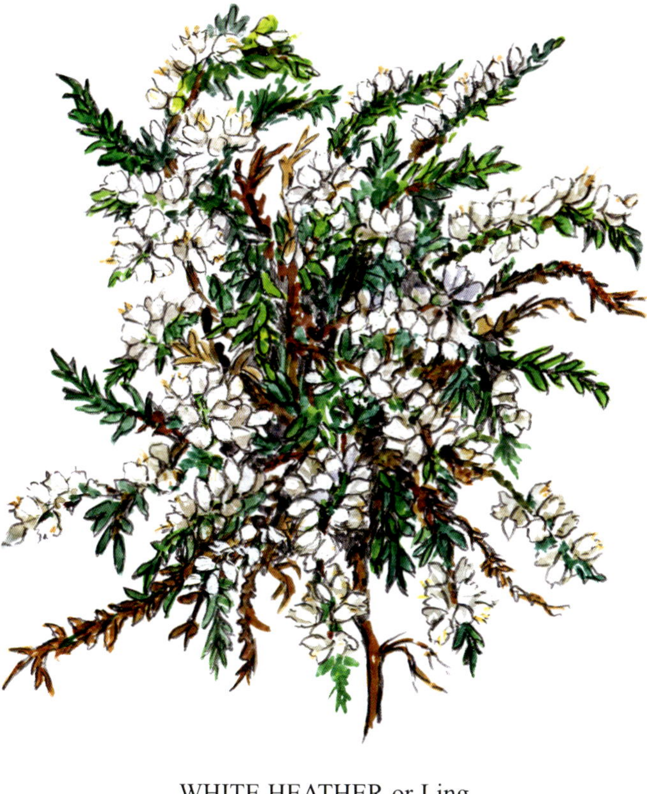

WHITE HEATHER or Ling

Calluna vulgaris *Family ERICACEAE*

Rarely the heather of the high hills produces a white plant. To find it will, of course, bring good luck!

Flowers from August to September.

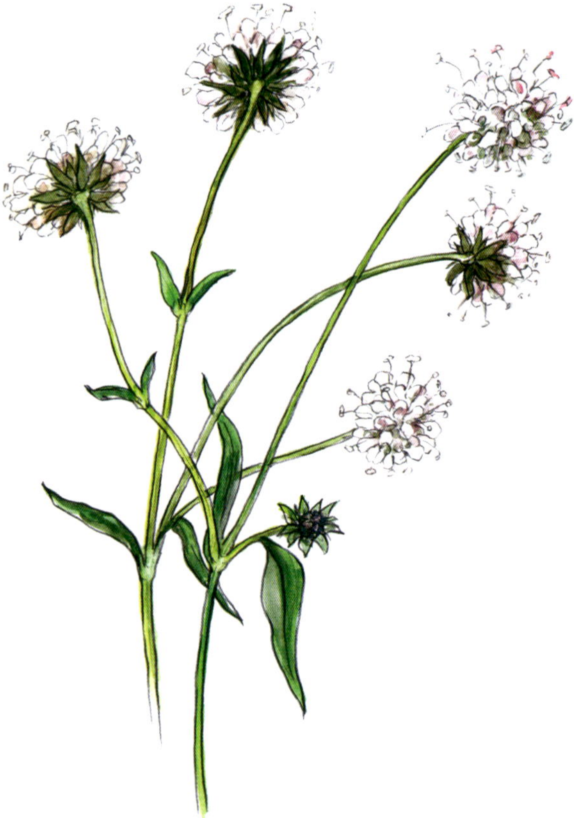

WHITE DEVILSBIT SCABIOUS

Succisa pratensis *Family DIPSACACEAE*

This is an occasional version of the common blue scabious in a white form. It prefers moist soil, damp meadows and woods.

Flowers from June to October.

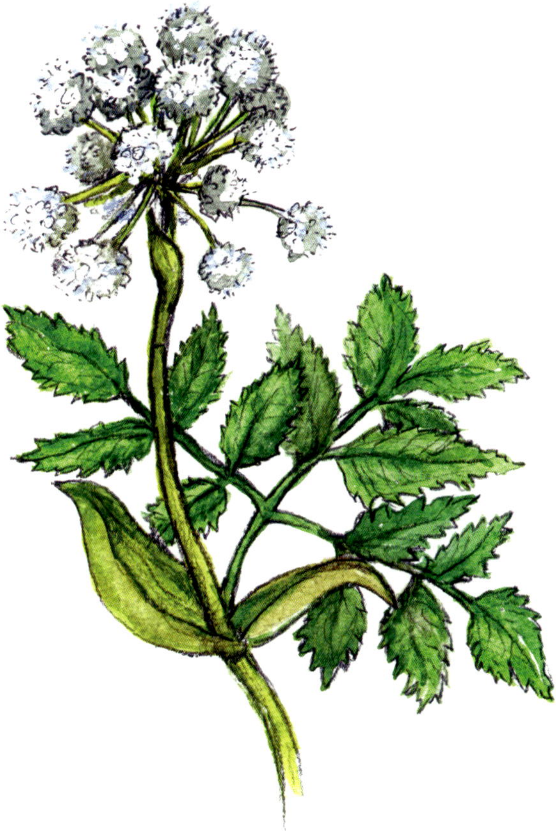

WILD ANGELICA

Angelica sylvestris *Family UMBELLIFERAE*

Common in damp woodlands and hedges. Notable are its sturdy, purple stems, and rounded flower head.

Flowers from June to September.

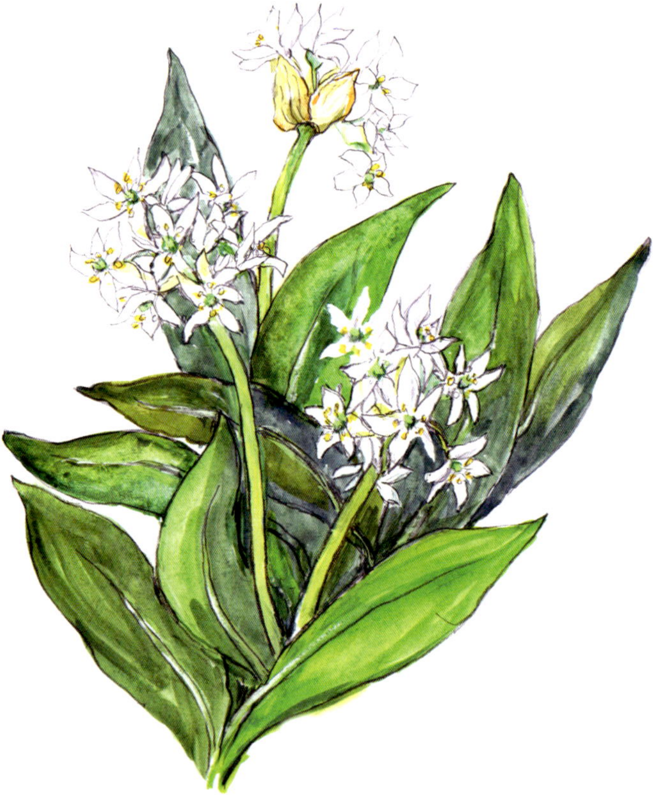

WILD GARLIC or Ramsons

Allium ursinum *Family LILLIACEAE*

With large glossy leaves this plant covers the woodland floor and shady banks, in the valley. The global heads of white flowers make a spectacular show, though some may find the garlic smell a bit overpowering. The leaves are edible.

Flowers from April to June.

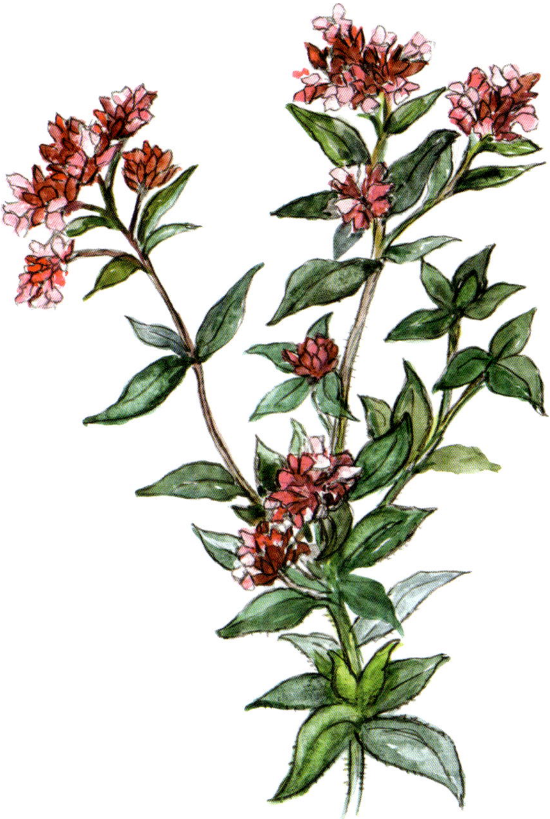

WILD MARJORAM

Origanam vulgare *Family LABIATAE*

This aromatic plant grows to eighteen inches, with branching slender stems. It has heads of loose, dark purple buds turning to a paler purple flower. It grows on dry alkaline soil on the hills.

Flowers July to September.

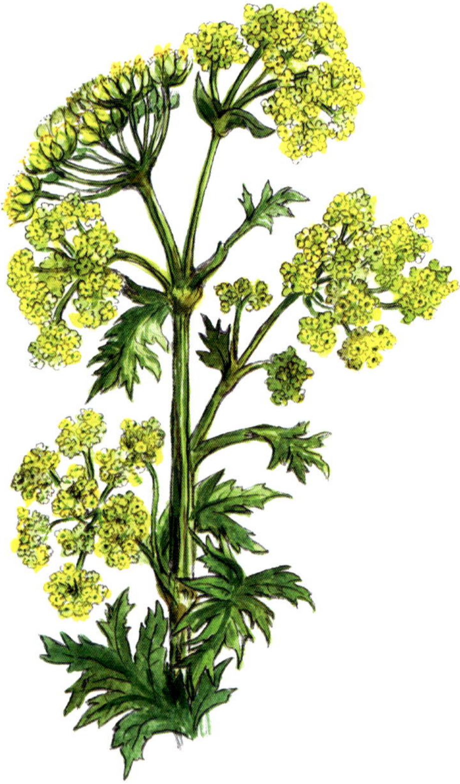

WILD PARSNIP

Pastinaca sativa *Family UMBELLIFERAE*

A rather hairy plant two to four foot high. It is the only yellow flowering umbellifer here, with spaced-out clusters of flowers on the stem heads. It is common along roadsides and dry grassland. It has a distinctive smell when crushed.

Flowers from July to September.

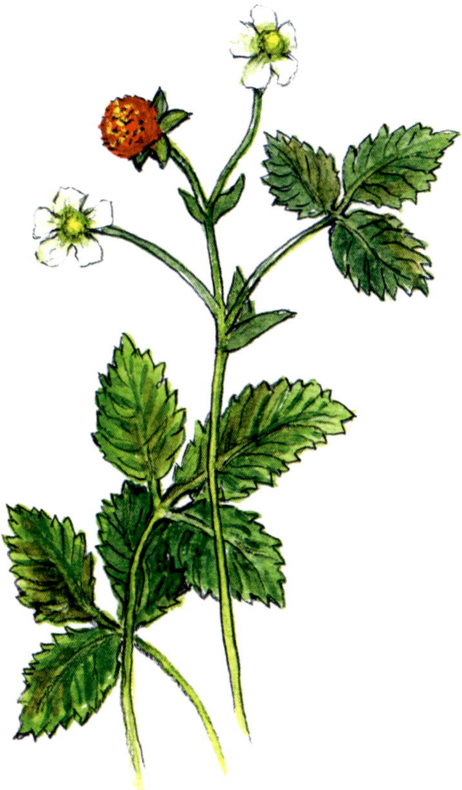

WILD STRAWBERRY

Fragaria vesca *Family ROSACEAE*

It looks like a miniature garden strawberry with rooting runners and trefoil leaves, unjoined at their base, which have deeply etched veins. The flowers are white with five petals, and the little fruits are delicious to eat.

Flowers from April.

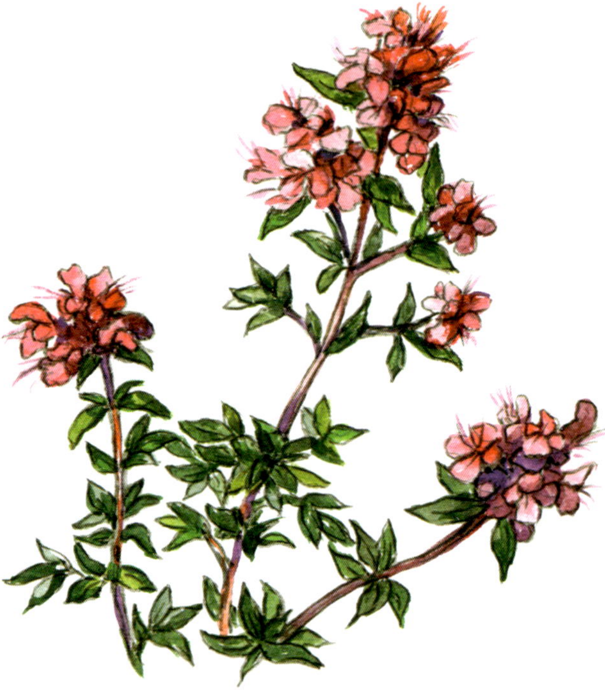

WILD THYME

Thymus serpyllum *Family LABIATAE*

This low, sweet smelling pink perennial grows on the hills in dry, stoney and grassy areas. It is matted with hairy stems and small dark green leaves.

Flowers from May to September.

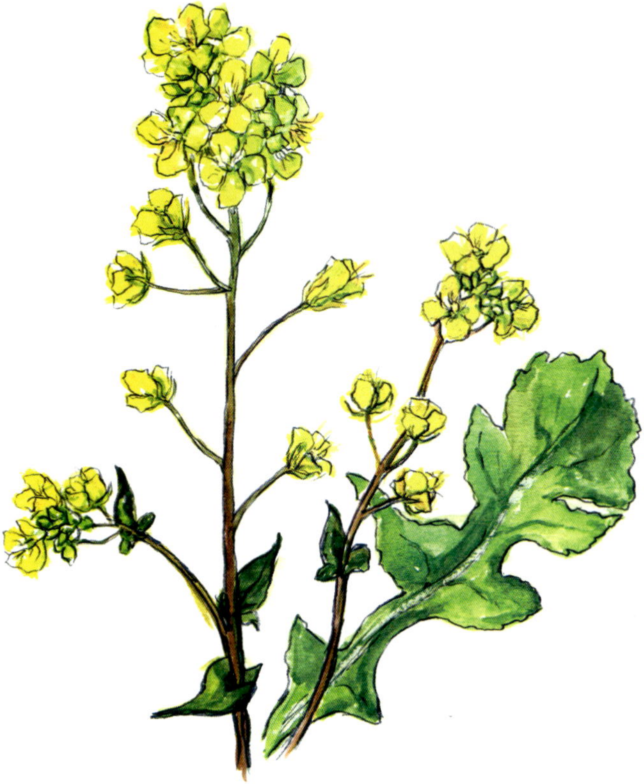

WILD TURNIP

Brassica lapa *Family CRUCIFERAE*

A tall annual with lobed leaves which are unstalked, and broader at the base. The bright yellow flowers branch from a naked stalk at the top of the plant. It grows in open, preferably bare, spaces.

Flowers April to September.

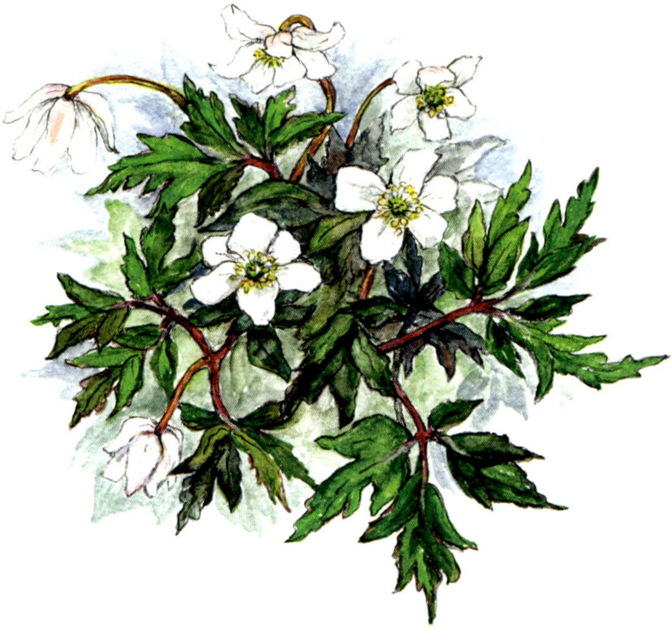

WOOD ANEMONE

Anemone nemorosa *Family RANUNCULACEAE*

In the spring this flower can be found carpeting the woodland floors. Its delicate white flowers and feathery leaves make it particularly attractive. Occasionally the flowers are tinged with pink, and can be found on relict woodland on open moorland pastures.

Flowers from March to May.

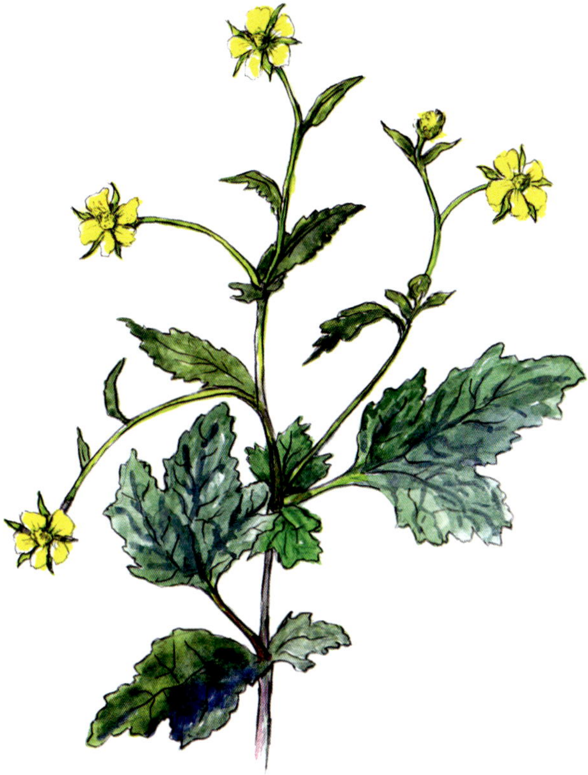

WOOD AVENS or Herb Bennet

Geum urbanum *Family ROSACEAE*

Though not confined to woods this yellow flower is found in hedges and shady places where it is damp. The roots, which have a clove-like smell, were once thought to protect a home from the devil.

Flowers from June to August.

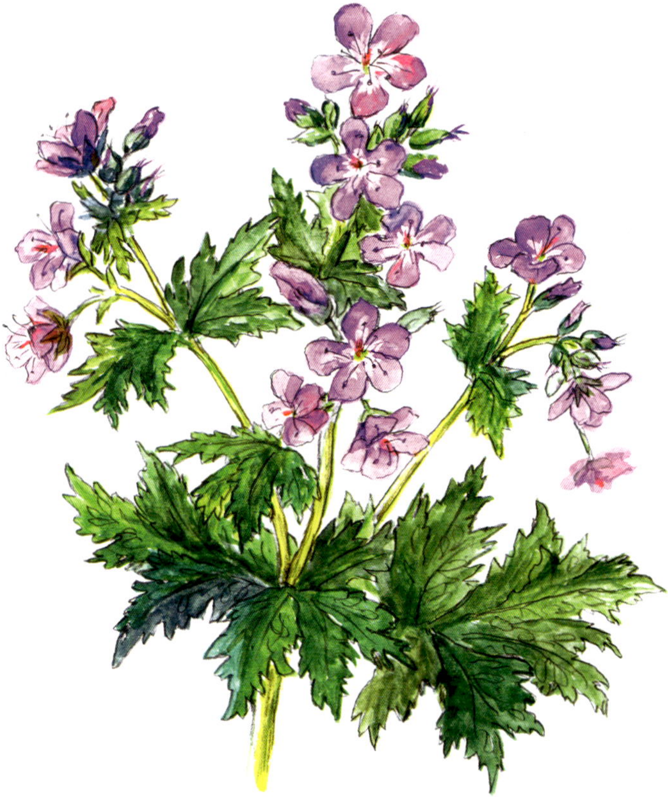

WOOD CRANESBILL

Geranium sylvaticam *Family GERANIACEAE*

Several delicate reddish purple flowers grow on fine stems at the top of the plant, from deeply serrated leaves which fan out around the stalk. It favours the North of England and Scotland.

Flowers from June to August.

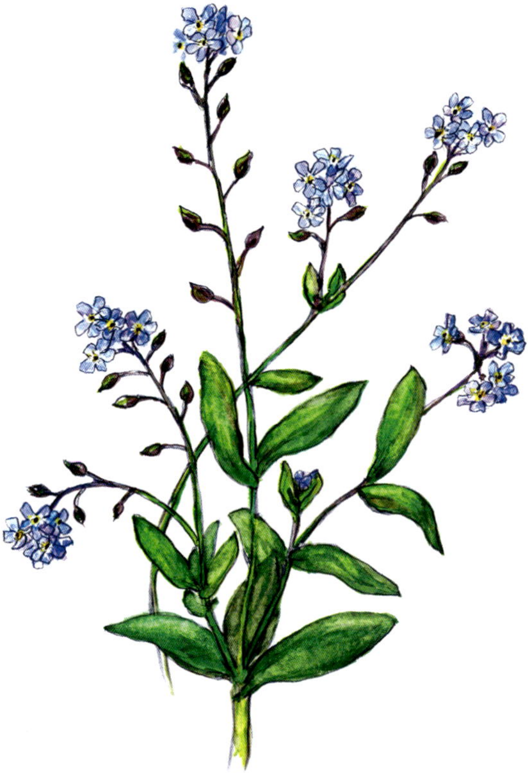

WOOD FORGET-ME-NOT

Myosotis sylvatica *Family BORAGINACEAE*

There are a number of forget-me-nots found locally, some very small and others, like this one, growing a foot or more high in woods and hedge banks. Its distinctive little cobalt blue flower is sometimes tinged with pink and has a yellow eye.

Flowers June to September.

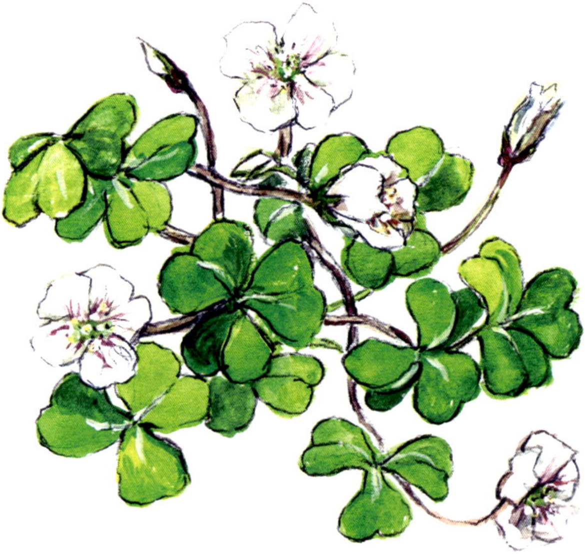

WOOD SORREL

Oxalis acetosella *Family OXALIDACEAE*

A creeping perennial with single white flowers with mauve veins, and trefoil leaves. It likes shady places, and can be found in woods and hedges.

Flowers from April to May.

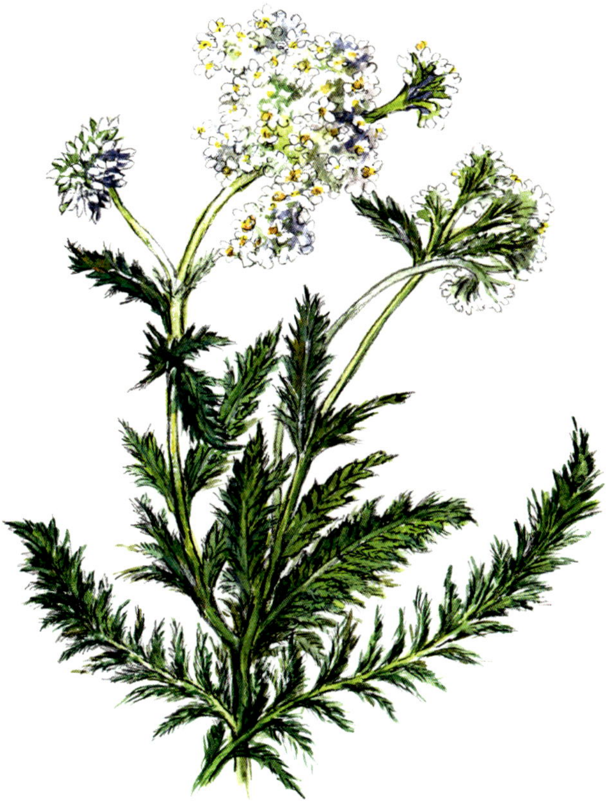

YARROW or Milfoil

Achillea millefolium *Family COMPOSITAE*

This flower grows from finely divided, feathery leaves. It has a strong stem and a head of small white flowers which have a pungent smell. It can be found along the valley roads and in fields.

Flowers from June to August.

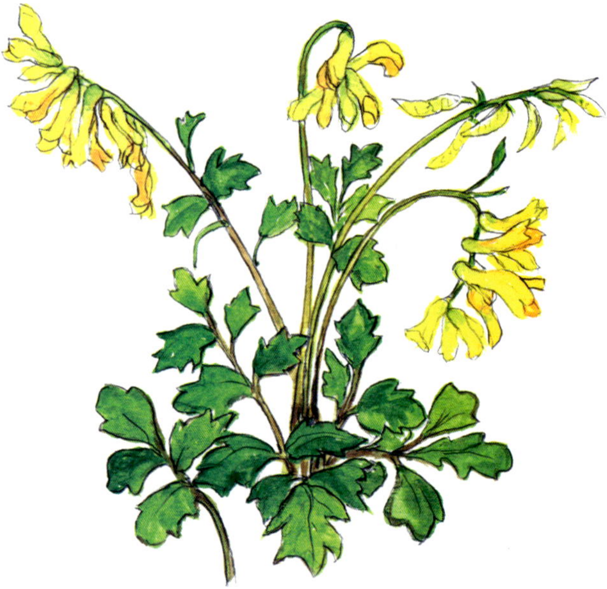

YELLOW CORYDALIS

Corydalis lutea *Family FUMERIACEAE*

This is a garden escape originally from southern Europe, which has spread happily over walls and in mortar cracks. Its trumpet-like yellow flowers all face the same side of the stem. The leaves are not unlike flat parsley.

Flowers from May to September

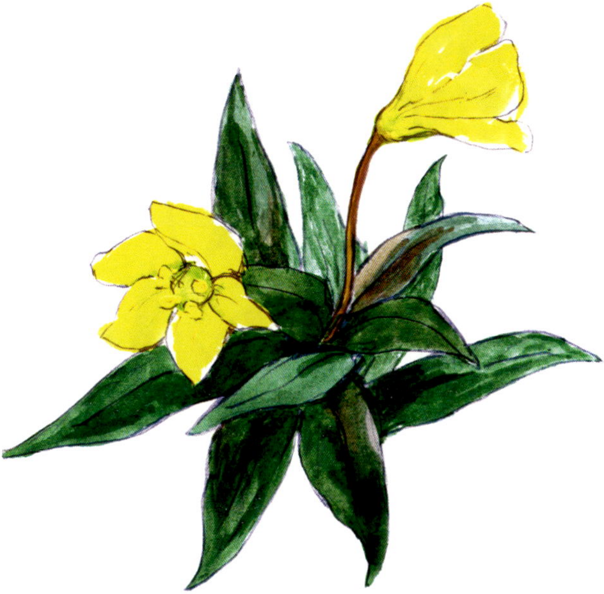

YELLOW MARSH SAXIFRAGE

Saxifraga hirculus *Family SAXIFRAGACEAE*

A delicate yellow flower, which is very rare, and grows in high spring flushes in the north of Britain. It sometimes has orange spots at the base of the petals. The flowers are borne singly on hairy red stems, rising from a rosette of leaves. Draining of spring flushes has caused a decline of this beautiful plant.

Flowers from June to August.

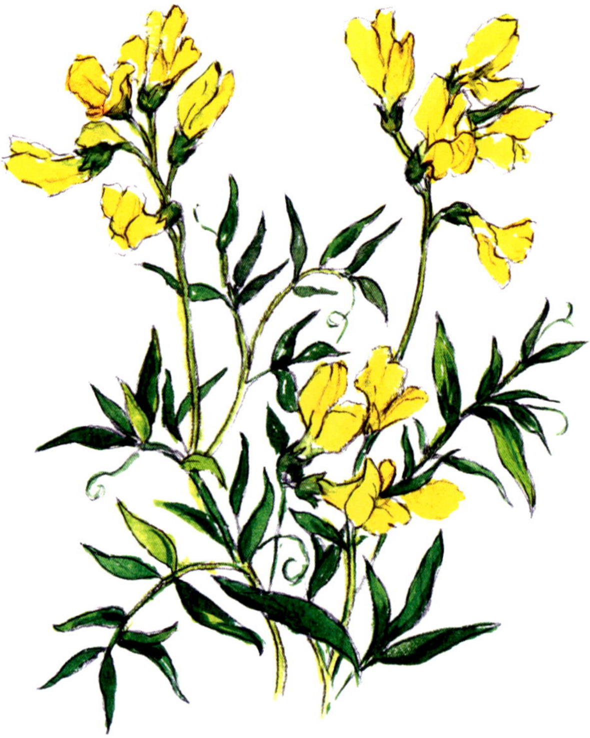

YELLOW MEADOW PEA or Yellow Vetchling

Lathyrus pratensis *Family LEGUMINOSAE*

This yellow pea grows in hedges and field borders throughout the valley. It scrambles over other plants, attached by tendrils from single pairs of narrow leaflets.

Flowers from June onwards.

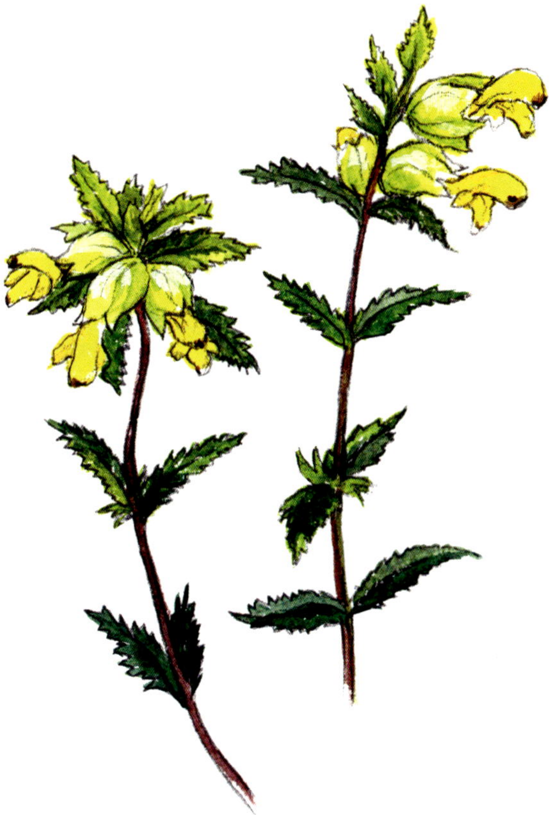

YELLOW RATTLE

Rhinanthus crista-galli *Family OROBANCHACEAE*

Unstalked, toothed, leaves grow in pairs opposite each other along the stalk. These yellow flowers grow in grassy places, and have flat, winged seeds which rattle inside when ripe.

Flowers from May to July.

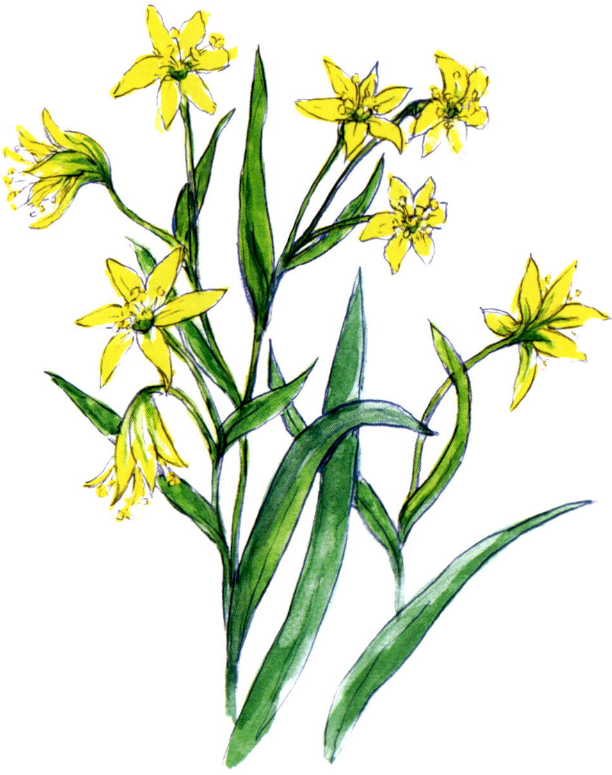

YELLOW STAR-OF-BETHLEHEM

Gagea lutea *Family LILIACEAE*

This rare delicate yellow flower, with six petals, flowers sparingly at the end of leafless stalks. The leaves are not unlike those of bluebells. It grows in damp and shady places and woods in the lower dale.

Flowers from March to April.

Acknowledgements

I wish to thank Tim Laurie and Stephen Eastmead of the Swaledale and Arkengarthdale Archaeology Group for their help in locating and recording the flowers illustrated here. A special thank you goes to Janet Eastmead for her help in identifying and providing Latin names for the specimens. Hayloft Publishing and The Yorkshire Dales National Park staff have been enthusiastic supporters, for which I am very grateful. I have referred to the following books for information in the short texts:

Collins: The Wild Flowers of Britain and Northern Europe
Collins Gem, Wild flowers
The Concise British Flora, W. Keble Martin.
The Oxford Book of Wild Flowers.
A Flora of Wensleydale, Deborah Millward

About the Author

JOCELYN CAMPBELL descends from a dales family which left for York in the late nineteenth century. Her parents and sister returned to settle in Swaledale and Arkengarthdale and she from early childhood spent annual holidays in the dales, to where she and her husband finally retired.

Coming from several generations of Swiss and French artists on her mother's side, Jocelyn trained as an artist herself, studying in London and Edinburgh colleges. She became a lecturer in Art in colleges of education in Scotland and at Stirlng University.

Once settled in the dales she has painted the landscapes and flora and has recently published, through the Swaledale and Arkengarthdale Archaeology Group (SWAAG), a book of drawings of the trees of Swaledale.

Although she does not consider herself to be a botanical artist, her delight in observing the wild flowers of Lebanon, when she and her family lived there, led her to publish a beautiful book of paintings of the flora of the region.

Her hope is that this book will stimulate interest in the especially abundant and beautiful flowers of the two dales.